Roll-out Racquetball

Other books by
CHARLES BRUMFIELD and JEFFREY BAIRSTOW

Off the Wall: Championship Racquetball for the
Ardent Amateur

Roll-out Racquetball

CHARLES BRUMFIELD
and
JEFFREY BAIRSTOW

THE DIAL PRESS
NEW YORK

Published by
The Dial Press
1 Dag Hammarskjold Plaza
New York, New York 10017

Copyright © 1982 by Charles Brumfield and Jeffrey Bairstow.

Manufactured in the United States of America

First printing

Library of Congress Cataloging in Publication Data
Brumfield, Charles.
  Roll-out racquetball.

  Includes index.
  1. Racquetball. I. Bairstow, Jeffrey, 1939–
II. Title.
GV1003.34.B78   796.34′3   81-17463
ISBN 0-385-27407-6   AACR2

Contents

Roll-out Racquetball

1

The Competitive Racquetball Player

In this book I'm going to talk about the rapidly changing components of today's racquetball game. I intend to evaluate new stroking styles, new tactics, and new strategies in the light of the classic ideas about the game, which were covered in my previous book, *Off the Wall* (The Dial Press, 1978).

Early racquetball players—my contemporaries—came in from other sports, so the techniques they used were primarily those they learned from their first sport, whether squash, tennis, or, as in my own case, paddleball. However, we now have a generation of players who have grown up with racquetball as their primary sport, and the techniques of the sport have changed radically. This book will, I hope, show you how to make the best of these new and exciting developments in racquetball and so improve your own game whether you are from my generation or have grown with the sport.

The Serve

My Philosophy of Serving In racquetball as it's played today, the serve is the major weapon. You should develop an effective arsenal of serves. You can be taught by someone more experienced, but this is only a stepping-stone to the second method of developing a variety of serves: experimenting on your own. The third way is to watch other players, not just the pros but all players, even novices. The novices' serves may be unorthodox, but they can be as effective as many of the pros' serves and even more surprising to your opponent. You should be able to master fifteen or twenty varieties of serves, motions, and zone positions. There are so many different kinds of opponents that you can never have too large a battery of serves up your sleeve. Everyone needs to develop his or her own portfolio of serves, so we'll start with serves in Chapter 2.

I recommend safe but aggressive second serves. Most players are ultraconservative about their second serves, yet they'll shoot a shoulder-high backhand. The second serve is just as important as the first in forcing a weak return.

The Power Forehand

The Power Backhand

To win at racquetball today, you'll also need power in your game. The generation of pure racquetball players—the kids who learned how to hit a racquetball almost as soon as they learned to walk—have developed their own techniques. While I was on top, I had a control game as a direct result of my earlier paddleball days. With well-placed finesse shots I was able to give my opponent the runaround until he dropped from exhaustion. But Marty Hogan's power game made me realize how effective power can be against the control player.

Today's Power Game

There are other factors which have made power effective: Racquetball is the most offensive of all the racquet sports because you don't have to worry about hitting into the net, into the tin, out of bounds, or off the table. The ball is faster and conditioning is less important, because the tiebreaker has been shortened from twenty-one to eleven points. Therefore, it's important for everyone to learn to hit with power, a topic we'll cover in Chapter 3 on the forehand and Chapter 4 on the backhand.

Just as the development of the jump shot revolutionized basketball, the power game has revolutionized racquetball. The young power players have shown everyone that they can hit with more power and more control both on the run and in the air.

The power game is here to stay, and older players can only reminisce about the good old days when opponents dropped dead from rushing around. But the advent of the passing game does not exclude the defensive overhead shots we'll be taking a look at in Chapter 5.

The New Strategies The old center-court theory was one that I myself helped to develop, but with the numerous changes in racquetball it has now become grossly outdated.

According to the center-court theory, the best place to be to cover any shot is dead center, because there you are equidistant from all four corners. In my center-court theory days, I thought I could shoot better from up front than from deep in the court.

But racquetball has become an execution game, not a retrieving one. When the ball travels faster, it's best to be deeper in the court for extra time to prepare for the shot. Players like Hogan wait in the back court and hit the ball at the last possible moment. But when Hogan hits the ball, he goes for a winner; he doesn't try to keep the ball in play.

I call my new strategy the moving-pocket defense. I assume that most shots will end up crosscourt. Therefore, I position myself in that area and so cover the shot much earlier and with less effort than the player who waits to see where the ball is going.

The Center-Court Strategy

You can also dictate your opponent's shot by your positioning during the rally. You can learn your opponent's favorite shots by watching his game or scouting before a match. And you can anticipate where most shots will go by watching your opponent's stroke. Chapter 6 gives you the full story on the new strategies of racquetball.

But there's more to winning racquetball than merely adopting a new strategy of play. Every opponent and every game are different, so you should develop game plans to suit your style of play and to counter other players. In Chapter 7 I'll show you how to work on your own game plans and I'll suggest ways of attacking various types of players.

The Game of Doubles

In the crowded confines of the racquetball court, doubles is both a demanding and a dangerous game. It's demanding because it calls for super teamwork and precise shotmaking at all times. Doubles is dangerous

The Game of Doubles

because four players wheeling around the court are like four bulls in a china shop—something is almost certain to get broken. Safe but fun doubles calls for more skill, I often feel, than the singles version of the sport.

In Chapter 8 I will cover the new strategies of doubles, the mental aspects of the game, and the particular shots that will make you a fearsome doubles player without maiming your teammate or your opponents for life.

And because mixed doubles poses a different set of problems, Chapter 9 will take a look at the major aspects of a game that I've learned a lot more about recently—since my marriage to another racquetball enthusiast.

Practice Makes Perfect Few racquetballers know exactly how, what, where, when, and with whom they should practice to perfect their game. Practicing involves a lot more than banging the ball around by yourself while you're waiting for your partner to show up.

What's needed is a goal. This is what makes the game fun, challenging, and in the end, rewarding. If you don't practice regularly you will never reach your full potential as a racquetball player.

To work toward a goal, you have to define it. Do this with your local teaching pro. He or she should work with you on the basic strokes and help you decide what style of play you should adopt.

Alternatively, you might watch the pros or the top amateurs in your area. If you have a fiery personality, you'll probably be more comfortable with an aggressive style of play. If you are the more analytical person, who spends time philosophizing about the game, the defensive style of play will probably fit you best. Chapter 10 will show you how to set your own goals and how to practice to achieve them.

Conditioning for Competition

Conditioning is extremely important if you want to be in top tournament shape. For example, for flexibility and warm-up I suggest arm circles, torso twists, cross-leg toe touches, leg overs, groin stretches, Achilles tendon stretches, jumping jacks, backward running, side shuffles, and skipping. And that's just for starters. You'll need cardiovascular conditioning, too. It's all covered in Chapter 11.

For those players who can't find time for a full conditioning schedule, I also have a miniprogram. Whichever regime you decide on, it's best to start with what you and your physician decide you can handle and then work up.

The Well-Equipped Racquetballer

The Competitor's Gear Although most of this book is devoted to getting you and your strokes in shape to play the competitive game, you can't afford to neglect your weapons. So the final chapter (12) I've devoted to racquets, shoes, balls, clothing, and all the other items you'll need to play a winning game.

2

Make Your
Serve a Weapon

The first step in making the most of your serve is to develop an awareness of what you can do with the serve. Step out on the court by yourself with a few balls, and turn your imagination loose.

Hit from every part of the service zone to different parts of the front wall. This will give you a true appreciation of what the ball will do under every conceivable serving situation. Then, through practice, you can make your racquet and body learn how to repeat the desired shot.

A second method is to have someone more experienced show you some new ideas on court. This information should only act as a seed from which your own ingenuity will produce serves that fit your physical and mental makeup.

A third method is to observe other players. Watch even B and C players who have had little or no formal instruction and have no preconceived notions of how to hit a drive serve or how to step into a Z serve. These players have created their own serves, and some are truly awesome.

The Setup

The Ball Bounce

The Backswing   The Forward Step

The next step is to select a group of serves to make peculiarly your own. It's impossible to learn all the possible variations in the serve, since there are an infinite number of angles to the court and a wide range of speeds of delivery. But too many people are satisfied with only two or three variations. Almost all players from the top pros down to novices have fallen into that trap.

Any diligent player should have fifteen or twenty varieties of serves, motions, and zone positions. This may seem a bit intimidating, but remember that during the serve you are in complete control of the shot and can use up to ten seconds to decide on your serve and where and how to hit it.

Of course there is one particular serve that would prove the most effective against a particular opponent

The Downswing   Wrist Cock

at one point of a game, but it might not be applicable in the next point, let alone against another opponent with different strengths and weaknesses.

So let me suggest serves which I think you ought to master. They should serve to whet your curiosity and help you explore types of serves on your own.

A good server should be able to beat the returner at his strength, normally his forehand. This will force your opponent into a situation where he will be unable to compensate for his weaker side (usually the backhand).

So my serving recommendations are specifically designed to be bold in that I suggest serving to the forehand of the receiver. The more practice you put in on serves to the forehand, the more weak returns you'll get in a match.

Ball Contact   The Follow-Through

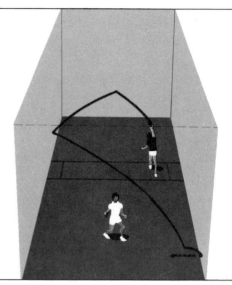

Fig. 1 The Deep Z Serve

The Z Serves The deep Z serve should be your bread-and-butter shot. The Z serves are those which hit the front wall, side wall, and floor before hitting a third wall (either another side wall or the back wall). The deep Z is sometimes referred to as the snap Z by more advanced players, the snap being the quick movement of the wrist as the server comes through the hitting zone. This snap gives greater velocity and deception, making the pace and direction of the serve difficult to read by the receiver.

Serve the deep Z about two feet from the side wall, with your left foot forward. The serve will travel from the front wall down the side wall and hit the floor in deep right court (Fig. 1), with spin from the surfaces struck in its flight.

Two other very effective serves can be used from the same starting position. They are the drive down the line and the hard V.

Both the drive down the line and the hard V take

Fig. 2 The Drive-Down-the-Line Serve   Fig. 3 The Hard V Serve

advantage of the short zone, the area just behind the short line, which is one of the most neglected service areas in the game.

The drive down the line (Fig. 2) is hit off the same motion as the deep Z, the only difference being the flatter angle of the racquet as it comes through the hitting area. Hit the ball with maximum force so that the receiver is deceived and thinks you are attempting a deep Z.

If hit well, the drive-down-the-line serve can surprise your opponent so that his reaction will be slow enough to allow the ball to bounce twice for a winning ace.

The hard V serve (Fig. 3) uses the same motion but goes the other way down the court and is particularly effective if your opponent is expecting a serve to the forehand. This serve is a drive to the backhand, but aimed again for the short zone, with the ball in the air as little as possible.

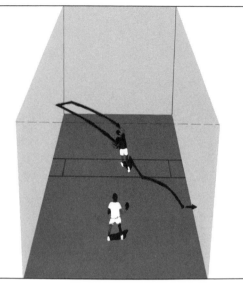

Fig. 4 The Short-Angle Z Serve

Serving to the short zone may be a new concept to you, since many players feel that a deep court rebound is the desired end of a Z serve. I have learned from bitter experience, however, that the weakest area from which to return a serve is the short zone. A ball in the short zone forces the receiver to strike the ball while moving forward rapidly, which eliminates virtually all his power, since he cannot get set for the ball.

Another serve to the short zone is the short-angle Z (Fig. 4). Technically, this is really not a Z, because it is designed to hit the floor twice before reaching the third wall. However, the path traveled by the ball is identical with the deep Z and the stroke is the same.

The trajectory is different in that the short-angle Z will strike front wall–side wall (hit low and hard) and hit the floor just behind the short line.

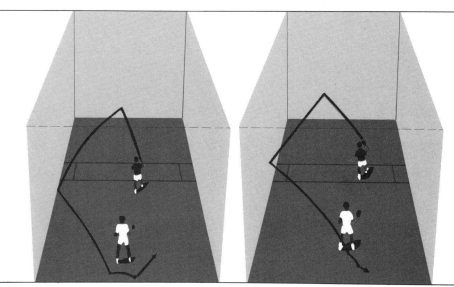

Fig. 5 The Jam-and-Fly Serve   Fig. 6 The Side-Wall-Jam Serve

The jam serves are struck so as to rebound directly **The Jam Serves**
into the center of the court at the receiver's body. Although many experts warn against serving down the
middle, the jam serves to the receiver's body can be
very effective.

I often favor the jam-and-fly serve (Fig. 5), because
it can tie a receiver in knots. Hit the ball with maximum
power right at the short line. The rebound will take the
ball nearly to the back wall, where its speed will cause
it to rebound and fly back into the center of the court.

The flight will make the receiver spin around in an
attempt to chase the ball down. Otherwise the receiver
will have to take the ball off the difficult short hop,
making any offensive return virtually impossible.

An alternative to the jam and fly is the side-wall-
jam serve (Fig. 6). Hit the side-wall-jam serve from the
center of the service zone. The ball will strike front
wall–side wall and rebound behind the server, directly
at the receiver. This should produce a weak return, be-

Fig. 7 The Wide Jam Serve (Backhand) Fig. 8 The Wide Jam Serve (Forehand) Fig. 9 The Surprise Jam Serve

cause the selection of a return cannot be made sufficiently fast by most receivers to handle the side-wall-jam serve properly.

Both the jam-and-fly and side-wall-jam serves can be hit to either side of the court, so they should both be hit from the center of the service zone. You can also hit the jam serve wide to either the forehand or backhand side.

In both cases the receiver will probably be too slow to get his entire body into the return, thereby reducing his power.

Note that the wide jam serves (Figs. 7 and 8) are hit from closer to the side wall, that is, from the same position as the Z and short-zone serves.

The final jam serve is the boldest of all—the surprise jam (Fig. 9). This is a ball hit right at your opponent. Most receivers figure the serve directly at them is the least likely to be used, so the surprise jam will catch them off balance. Make sure to use plenty of power

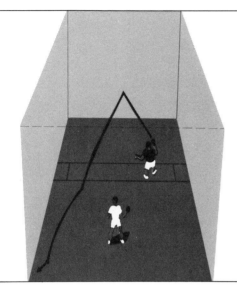

Fig. 10 The Pure V Drive Serve

and be sure the receiver is not expecting it. If your opponent can take this ball off the back wall, he or she will have a clear path down the right side of the court.

Most of the traditional serves are not effective in racquetball as it's played today. The game has changed, but the serves have not.

    Take, for example, the pure V drive (Fig. 10), the staple of power servers everywhere. When an athlete such as Marty Hogan winds up and blasts the pure V drive toward a hapless receiver's backhand, the result is often an ace; otherwise the serve forces a weak return. But for those of us who are not blessed with 140-mph boomers, the drive serve can be beaten.

    The drive is vulnerable for three reasons: First, most players sacrifice accuracy in going for maximum

The Traditional Serves

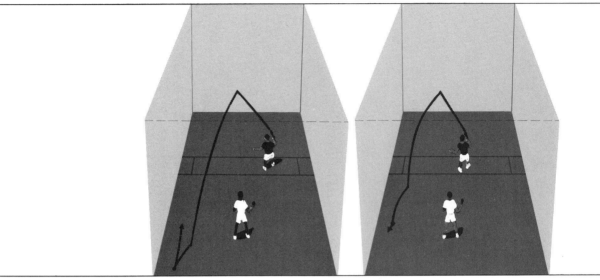

Fig. 11 The Drive-and-Fly Serve   Fig. 12 The Garbage Serve

power, which usually results in too many short serves. Even the best players have trouble getting this serve over the line often enough to make it effective.

Secondly, the drive is often hit too high, especially after a run of short serves. Any ball that hits over two feet high on the front wall will rebound off the back wall when struck with maximum force. That's an easy sitter for the receiver.

Thirdly, the pure V drive is often mis-hit to drop in no-man's-land—too wide, but not wide enough where it is. This is another easy return for the receiver.

An alternative to the pure V drive is the drive-and-fly serve (Fig. 11). This is another serve that you some-times see by accident as a pure V drive is mis-hit and the result is a ball that comes off the back wall so fast that it rebounds to the short zone before the receiver can catch up to it.

If the drive-and-fly serve can be used as part of your repertoire it can be devastating. The drive-and-fly serve is struck with maximum velocity about two and one-half feet high on the front wall so that it lands near the back wall and flies back toward front court. Be sure the drive-and-fly serve does not hit the side wall, where the flight of the ball will be slowed enough to make it a setup.

What usually occurs after the short attempt at a booming pure V drive is the garbage serve (Fig. 12). The garbage serve is frequently used as the second serve by both pros and top amateurs. It's effective because it requires the receiver to hit the ball from chest or shoulder height, where it's tough to put much power into it.

Of course the garbage serve will rarely give you an ace or winner, since it is designed to allow a return. The properly hit garbage serve does not touch either the back or side walls and is always over waist-high to the receiver.

The garbage serve must be hit at a maximum of

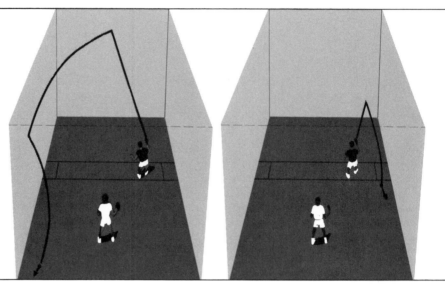

Fig. 13 The Lob Serve   Fig. 14 The Half-Speed Dying-Quail Serve

three-quarters of top speed and preferably nearer to half speed. You can also vary the garbage serve by serving down the line.

Ten years ago the lob serve (Fig. 13) was probably the most used delivery. The lob can be nearly impossible to intercept in midair and often, when catching the side wall, dies behind the receiver. With today's faster ball, the lob is not often used, but it can be effective as a change of pace.

The Spin Serves Probably the best spin serve is a close relative to the garbage serve, which I call the half-speed dying-quail serve (Fig. 14). This serve is hit with a combination of backspin and sidespin (a three-quarters spin rather like a pitcher's curve ball). The ball should be served so that it just clears the short line, where it will take a

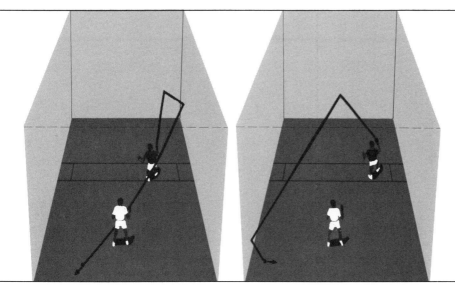

Fig. 15 The Spin-Jam Serve   Fig. 16 The Deep Spin Serve

short, quaillike hop and then die. The resulting rush and lunge to retrieve the ball by the receiver should be a pleasant sight to the server.

Another effective spin serve is the spin-jam (Fig. 15) serve, originally used as a doubles serve. The spin-jam serve confuses righty/lefty teams by hitting the back wall in the middle of the court. The spin then takes effect and causes great confusion. The spin-jam serve can also be an effective singles serve, and the spin can be hit with either inside or outside sidespin.

A rarely used spin serve is the deep spin serve (Fig. 16). The deep spin serve is hit with extreme underspin and aimed directly at the crack at about three-quarters court. What happens then is an open question. If the ball hits the floor first and then the side wall, it will bounce up high into the receiver's chest. If the ball strikes the side wall first and then the floor, it tends to die near the crack.

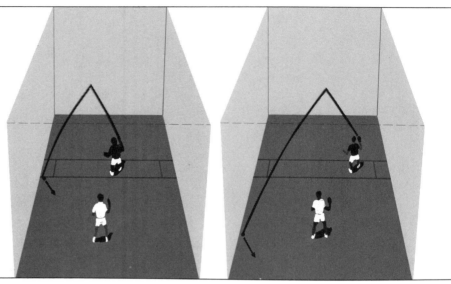

Fig. 17 The Angle-Crack Serve   Fig. 18 The Deep Angle-Crack Serve

The Crack Serves That brings us to the most difficult of offensive serves—but the ones with the potential for greatest rewards—the crack serves. When the ball lands in the crack, it is almost always an outright winner.

The angle crack (Fig. 17) is the traditional crack serve. The ball is hit low so the point of contact with the side wall is only about one or two inches high and about a foot in front of the short line. The reason this is one of my favorites is that the odds are with the server. If you serve it shorter than intended, it's a short serve. If you serve it slightly longer than you intended, it's still an effective serve. The key is the angle. As long as the target on the side wall is the same, only the angle of rebound off the side wall (if you don't get a perfect crack) will differ. The angle-crack serve is good from either side and to either side of the court.

The deep angle-crack serve (Fig. 18) is an attempt to get the ball behind your opponent to hit the crack in deep court. It is almost impossible to return, whether or not it hits the crack perfectly. There is much margin for error in deep angle-crack serves. This is hitting a short-zone serve, which, as we have seen, can be very effective.

If you miss the crack deep, your serve will either be long or will come around behind your opponent, where it will still be a tough serve to return. Most power players feel the crack serve attempts are worth the risk. As long as you're careful, the results can add eight to ten points to your game almost overnight.

3

Hit the Power Forehand

Racquetball style is in a state of continual evolution. Ten years ago there were no "true" racquetball players—players who had grown up with the sport. The players excelling in early racquetball were for the most part converts from other racquet sports. From these divergent backgrounds, it's no surprise that the styles of the early greats were many and varied. Even the actual swing mechanics of the leading players were profoundly affected by their preracquetball sports endeavors.

During the early to mid seventies I gradually refined the principles of control racquetball. This was based on the ceiling-ball/hypotenuse offense and gradually became the infamous "tour of the court" offense, in which I would keep the ball in play until my opponent dropped dead from exhaustion.

My playing philosophy in those days was similar to Chris Evert's. In her defensive baseline game of tennis,

Chris returns every ball and lets her opponents make the mistakes. She literally wears her opponents down.

The swing I used back then naturally fitted the style I had chosen to use—a straight-back, straight-through motion that minimized error. A short, punching stroke won many a point front court and midcourt, where most of the scoring was done in those days. Even then, however, my peers were starting to use the strokes of the power game that has dominated recently.

The young lions who had come up whaling at the ball were still doing so and winning with it. Marty Hogan was able to combine, at a very early age, awesome power and incredible recovery. Hogan, of course, is not the only youngster in racquetball today who shoots from the hip.

The reasons for the domination of power are several:

1. Racquetball is the most offense- and power-oriented of all racquet games. Less accuracy is required in comparison to other racquet sports, where the slugger is hampered by a net, or a tin, or constricting sidelines and baselines.

2. Young players of today, since they have learned racquetball first, are developing racquetball swings and not modifying tennis, paddleball, or squash swings. They are demonstrating the technical ability to crush the ball beyond all expectations of the earlier era.

3. The quality of today's ball, which is substantially faster than its ancestor, has been instrumental in shifting the emphasis toward power.

4. Glass courts have markedly decreased the depth perception of the contestants. This works against the control player, because he requires five or six well-hit shots in a rally to move his opponent around.

5. The tiebreaker has removed much of the conditioning required for a full three-game match. The power player has the distinct advantage again.

I believe the next swing of the pendulum will occur when there are hundreds of youngsters who can hit with power on both the backhand and forehand sides. All-court ability will then decide championships. Superior conditioning, court leadership, the ability to set the pace, and pressure play will once again take their well-deserved places in the arsenal of a champion.

The Production of Power

Isaac Newton would be proud of Marty Hogan, for Hogan demonstrates Newton's formula for power: Force (or power) is equal to the weight of the object (the racquet) times the square of the speed. In layman's terms, take the weight of the racquet, multiply it by the speed with which the racquet is moving, and multiply it again by the speed, and that's your power.

Since the speed term of the equation is multiplied by itself, it's obvious that racquet speed is the single most important factor in the production of power. The faster you can make the racquet move, the harder the ball will be struck and the more power you'll get.

The formula would seem to indicate that a heavier racquet would create more power. However, a heavier racquet would be harder to swing, so the racquet head speed would be lower. You can increase the power ratio by playing with a lighter racquet. The faster you swing the racquet, the more power you will generate and the greater the speed of the ball will be.

I feel that two factors account for racquet head

speed—strength (25 percent) and technique (75 percent). Maximum power means maximum use of all parts of your body—legs, hips, torso, shoulders, arm, forearm, and wrist. All these parts play a crucial role in generating and transferring power to the racquet head.

Power Needs Timing   When I first started experimenting with ripping the ball, I often found the result to be less power rather than more. All my body parts were flying around but they rarely arrived in the hitting area together. That's the secret: precise timing.

Bill Tilden expressed his thoughts on timing in his 1923 book, *Match Play and the Spin of the Ball:* "There is a fraction of a second when ball and body are in such a juxtaposition that if the ball is struck then the speed and pace are increased over any other time of playing. That is the moment when the weight of the body crosses the center of balance in a forward movement, simultaneously with the ball in its backward flight, and the stroke and ball meet. Only by this forward movement of the body weight at the exact moment of striking the ball is it possible to acquire maximum power. That is perfect timing."

I've heard many an instructor tell a young player that his or her shot is not reaching the maximum because the student is swinging too hard. The student is often not swinging too hard but using poor timing. The larger body parts—the legs, hips, and shoulders—have to start milliseconds before the less bulky elements—the arm, forearm, and wrist—to arrive at the right place for maximum power.

I like to think of the proper swing as building from the ground up. The legs must release, starting the swing. This is called stepping into the ball. Then come the drive and torque of the hips. Next the torso and diaphragm, then shoulder, arm, forearm, and wrist, in that order.

What must be kept in mind is that although a pro may look smooth, his swing really is not. Each body part jerks or buggywhips in turn, producing the torque that eventually creates racquet head speed. A player who mistakenly tries to make his swing smooth will weaken his stroke. The power swing is like the crack of a bullwhip, the snap of a towel, the flip of a playing card, the whip of a Frisbee toss. The common denominator in each of these motions is the efficient production of tremendous speed and a recoil torque rather than a smooth flowing motion. Because of the recoil, tremendous results are created with very little apparent effort.

A Long Arc for Racquet Speed

As in golf, the longer the arc, the greater the power that is generated. In golf, the player has the luxury of choosing a longer club when he needs to generate a bigger arc. In racquetball, the movement of body parts must be lengthened. This includes hip turn, shoulder and torso turn, arm reach, and elbow position.

Golfers today are using a principle I call coil and recoil. Rather than a full, loose turn, the golfer now uses a tight torque movement that is not as long but is much faster. That is the key to racquet speed. In racquetball, the modern power player has extended the

The Backswing   The Body Turn   The Downswing

coil-and-recoil theory to both the hips and shoulders. These large body parts are relatively ponderous and can't be turned very quickly over a great distance. They must be torqued or recoiled in a short, explosive move.

In racquetball, the large arc, which gives the racquet sufficient distance to build to maximum speed, is created by elbow position. The flying elbow creates a loop or pendulum swing rather than the simple straight-back, straight-through swing that I used for years.

The advantages of the loop are twofold. First, rhythm is much easier to create and maintain because the racquet never stops once the backswing is initiated. Second, much more power is created. At the top of the backswing in the straight-back, straight-through swing, the speed of the racquet head is a cool zero. In the loop swing we have already built up speed and are thus contributing to power.

The next stage in power development is the pronation or rotation of the forearm. If you examine pho-

Wrist Cock   Ball Contact   The Follow-Through

tos of a big hitter just after contact, you'll see that the
hitting surface is pointing directly upwards. If the shot
was successful, it's obvious that the racquet face was
not in that position a moment before—at impact. What
you are seeing is the result of pronation of the forearm. Not only should the forearm coil and recoil
through the ball as if you were slapping someone in
the face, but it should open and close using the same
coil-and-recoil motion to add another snap to the ball.
This additional movement takes delicate timing.

The wrist snap is the final link in this chain reaction. Some players feel that the wrist snap is the prin-
cipal source of power. This is not so. In most good
power swings the wrist snap is primarily directional.
My swing experiments indicate that the elbow snap and
forearm torquing are the main sources of power, but
to be a true power player you must use all your re-
sources—including wrist snap.

Where to Make Contact The proper hitting zone is an area of much dispute among today's racquetball pros. For years, teachers have insisted on contacting the ball off the front foot on the forehand. I think that's hogwash. I believe that the proper release point is in line with the hitting shoulder. My experiments in racquetball have shown me that the ball remains squashed on the strings for a certain amount of time. Therefore, your hitting zone should be slightly deeper than was previously thought.

The incorrect front-foot theory has certainly ruined the power potential of many a swing. If contact is made that far forward you will not really be hitting the ball but rather utilizing a modified push. That's like an athletically inexperienced girl trying to throw a ball. She releases the ball too late and too far forward—and so is forced to push or shotput the ball rather than throw it properly.

One good indication that you're hitting the ball too far forward relative to your hitting shoulder will be a distinct tendency to hit crosscourt. Remember, my hitting-shoulder theory is applicable to the straight-ahead shot. If you wish to hit crosscourt, then you should contact the ball a little further out in front. Conversely, the pinch (side wall–front wall) should be contacted a little deeper. All this assumes the same stance, of course.

In addition to releasing the ball off your hitting shoulder, for maximum power you should strike the ball at your arm's distance from your hitting shoulder joint. Don't let the ball jam you. If you are cramped, you'll be forced to bend at the elbow while making contact, which will shorten your arc and reduce your power potential tremendously.

For maximum power you should move your weight from your back foot to your front foot during the forward swing. However, don't allow your upper torso to move too far forward or you'll lose your torque. The upper body must remain slightly behind your lead leg for maximum power.

Move Your Weight

Your head should tuck and actually move back during the power swing. If your head lunges forward, the built-up muscle tension in all other parts of the swing could be ruined. However, I feel that your weight should certainly not finish 90 percent on the front foot as is often taught. At one point in the swing, directly after your back leg drive release, the weight transfer is probably 80 percent complete, but the weight then transfers back toward the back foot, leaving the distribution about 60–40 between front and back foot.

Many of the techniques that are used in racquetball are a result of the former champions' experience in other racquet sports, particularly tennis. So let's take the forehand stroke and stepping technique in tennis and analyze them to see if they're proper for racquetball.

Footwork for Power

When you're hitting the ball in tennis, the rule is to move toward the shot. For example, to hit a shot down the right sideline you step with the foot furthest from the ball in the direction of the ball. So if I were standing facing the net at the baseline as my opponent hit a ball down my right alley, my first move would be a stepover with my left foot. That's now taught in racquetball, too. Many instructors recommend that you move your body sideways to a shot along the right wall, have your left foot across your right foot to control the shot, and then hit the ball off your front foot.

However, I believe maximum power and accuracy come from striking the ball not off the front foot but off the hitting shoulder from an upright position, which, in most cases, is closer to the back foot. I also believe that stepping first with the foot that is furthest from the ball is a poor movement for most of the shots in racquetball.

Your best bet is to make the first step a pivot, with the right foot to the right wall first, in a ministep. So if the ball hits the short-angled crack in front of you, you will have a better chance to return it. The crack ball is a situation that obviously would not happen in tennis. But in a four-wall racquetball court, the interior jam ball is one of the more difficult shots to handle, especially at the novice level. So if you step with your right foot first, and the ball jams you, you will at least get a clear swing.

If the ball continues to go down the right side, your next step is with your left foot, giving you a good chance to catch the ball even with your body in a square position. This is probably the optimum position to contact the ball.

The third step, if necessary, when the ball gets deep and dangerous on you, would be to step back with your right foot, hitting with an open stance similar to that of Bjorn Borg hitting a topspin forehand off his back foot.

Not only can you step back farther and deeper and hit with greater ease, but this footwork also eliminates the problem of cramping with the stepover method. A tight shot will not let you hit crosscourt and stop you from getting weight into the shot. If you step back with your right foot, you can hit into the side wall, down the line, or crosscourt with equal ease. If you throw your upper body forward as you step back and get most of your weight into the shot, you can generate virtually maximum power on any difficult gets from deep court.

4

Hit the Power Backhand

Most of us struggle with the backhand because we have had very little practice in using our strong side arm from the weaker side of the body.

Most youngsters throw baseballs and footballs, shoot basketballs, and hit golf balls and baseballs all from the right side. The body is simply more used to functioning from that side. Does that mean you are limited forever to that weak backhand? No. You have to start establishing some positive muscle memory from the wrong side.

Many teachers feel that, anatomically, the backhand is actually simpler because the follow-through goes away from the body and toward the target area, whereas the forehand requires a stroking motion across the body.

Many players have a much more powerful forehand than backhand. I believe, however, that the backhand can be every bit as powerful as the forehand.

A major reason for the lack of power on the backhand is the length of the swing. A golfer will choose a longer club when he needs to cover a greater distance. The longer the club, the longer the potential arc of the swing. Most people have a long swing on their backhand, but unfortunately most of that is on the follow-through.

If you are wondering why your backhand shots almost limp toward the front wall, the answer is simple—the arc of your swing prior to contact is probably too short. The racquet head doesn't have time to build up speed, and therefore, little power is produced.

Most club players and many pros hit the ball harder crosscourt because they are contacting the ball later in the swing, and so using more of what is usually wasted follow-through power. Swing arc is the key concept. Build a repeating swing with a big arc as though you were snapping a towel and you'll have all the power you'll ever need.

Tests show that the upright pendulum loop swing creates the largest arc. Not only is the arc wider than in the traditional straight-back, straight-through method, but the loop permits a continuous buildup in racquet head speed, because the head is never stationary, as it is at the top of the backswing in the traditional method.

The Loop Backhand Swing Let's take a look at the components of the loop backhand swing:

1. Continuous motion. Once you start the backswing, the racquet head should never stop moving. The path of the swing should look like the swing of a pendulum; it flattens out only in the hitting area.

2. Height. The higher your racquet reaches on your loop, the farther it has to drop and the more power will be built up. The hitting elbow must also reach very high and you should get the feeling you are lifting up with your upper diaphragm and shoulders. Swing almost as if you were taking a deep breath.

3. Depth. The deeper in your stance your racquet reaches, the more arc is created, and the easier it is to flatten out the hitting zone naturally while still maintaining speed. Depth is not as important as height, particularly at the upper level of the game. The reason is simple—the better your opponent, the more shots he'll force you to hit in the back corners. The closer you get to the back wall, the more embarrassing a deep flat swing will be.

4. Shoulder turn. A huge shoulder turn is used on the backhand. This, more than any other factor, is the obstacle that I have to overcome to make my backhand what I'd like it to be some day. The shoulder turn is absolutely essential, but only those who have a good tennis or squash background really do it well.

The Backhand Grip

Most racquetball teachers recommend a grip change when hitting a backhand. The change closes the face of the racquet to compensate for the different angle of the wrist and forearm relative to the forehand. So players often use an Eastern forehand grip for forehand strokes and an Eastern backhand grip for backhand strokes, as in tennis. However, many pros are now us-

The Setup

The Backswing

The Downswing

ing one grip for both forehand and backhand. Marty Hogan, for example, feels that there is not enough time in the fast pace of pro play to make a grip change, particularly on service return and when playing up front.

But even Hogan cannot change the laws of physics, which cause the ball to go where the plane of the racquet face directs it. To keep his racquet face square to the intended line of flight of the ball, Hogan inverts his forearm and wrist on the backswing and uses only a minimum rotation of the forearm and wrist opening and closing on the downswing.

In Hogan's case, the position of his wrist and forearm (and not the conventional closed Eastern grip) give the ball its flat trajectory. The traditional grip makes it difficult to hit with pace, particularly on waist-high shots, without rolling the wrist and forearm over the ball. That's tough to do and maintain consistency.

Ball Contact   The Follow-Through   Recovery

As you begin your backswing, your wrist should turn **The Backswing**
under. This has two effects: First, you'll use a looping
motion; not only will your shoulder and arm be involved in this pendulum-style swing, but the forearm,
wrist, and hand will also trace out their own mini-loop-
ing parabola. Secondly, if the ball comes too fast and
gets inside your normal contact position, the tendency
is to lift or cut the ball very severely and so hit the ball
too high on the front wall. If you close your racquet on
your backswing, you'll be able to keep the ball low.

You should contact the ball maybe six inches behind **The Contact**
your hitting shoulder. You should be thinking in terms **Zone**
of releasing the ball off your hitting shoulder.
    The biggest error I see when watching all levels of

play is players contacting the ball too far forward. This means the ball cannot be hit hard and you're not using your power.

Try to keep your body and arm moving together. This allows your body weight to be transmitted to the head of the racquet. When you take a backswing, don't let your arm go back on its own. You should firm up the connecting muscles in your upper arm so that your shoulder pulls your arm back and forward. If you don't do this, the power from the movement of your body dissipates and you have to swing much harder to hit the ball hard.

Watch the Ball Ever since I was a teenage paddleball player, I've always heard the phrase "Watch the ball." But it's only now at the late stages of my career that I truly understand what this phrase means. Although photos clearly showed that at impact I was watching the target and not the ball, I always felt that I was watching the ball. The same was true of my fellow pros. Watching the ball doesn't mean that. It means what it says, watch the ball. Use peripheral vision to see your opponent and get a fix on where you are on the court at all times. Remember, only the ball is moving, not the spot you are aiming at on the wall.

Eye contact is a particular problem on the backhand. The impulse to look at the target area prevents players from doing the two things necessary to produce power—use a very large shoulder turn and let the ball get into the proper hitting zone. If you turn your shoulders, it's very difficult to see your target area.

Most people swing when they can see both the ball and the target area together, and that's often too soon.

In addition, looking up too soon will open up your shoulder too early. If you turn your shoulder even a little, it virtually forces you to hit crosscourt.

The more weight you can get behind the backhand, **Get in Position** the more pace your shot will have. Use your knees. Flex as you loop into the ball and lift at impact so you use the hitting power trapped in your thighs and rear end.

If you lift properly with your legs and rear and then with your upper torso, you will feel that you're leaving the ground! This is the proper motion.

One common mistake made by keen players is to stay low throughout the swing. If you do that, you can use only your arm and wrist to supply power. But if you use your legs properly, you'll work hard only to swing easier.

You also want your weight moving into the shot as you move into the contact zone. However, just prior to impact, the knees and upper torso should actually shift backward slightly to accommodate the power of the racquet now flashing through the ball. This will add the final zip to your new power backhand.

5

Use Your Overhead Shots

When the ball is waist-high or above, for most players there is only one choice: to hit a defensive ceiling ball and wait for a better opportunity to score. But I believe we'd better look for other alternatives to keep pace with today's high-powered game.

I originally developed the ceiling ball to counter players who could hit down on a high ball. The ceiling shot would place the ball a little bit farther back, so my opponents had to go defensive. Thus the game evolved around an exchange of defensive shots up and down the left wall until the ball popped out of the side wall. Then I would win the rally with what I call a hypotenuse shot (from the left wall I would hit the ball into the right front corner with my forehand). I got away with that strategy because few players had an offensive overhead.

Two factors conspired to defeat my ceiling ball play. First, the fast ball all but eliminated the ceiling shot because of the difficulty in keeping it from popping off the back wall for an easy setup. Next, the notion of hitting the ball with the overhead developed as part of the overall offensive attitude of the game. Today the ceiling ball, not the overhead, is the low-percentage shot. A ceiling shot has to be perfectly executed or else you'll give the other guy a setup. The easiest shot in the game is a setup off the back wall, which is exactly what most ceiling shots become when using a fast ball.

So the player who can play the ball offensively from shoulder high is the player who will win today. Marty Hogan's shoulder-high backhand has virtually revolutionized the game of racquetball.

I feel that the manufacturers will eventually have to slow the ball down. When we have slow balls, the overhead will become even more important, because then the ceiling ball will return as a viable shot. Of course, when the ball starts going up to the ceiling again, the players who can bring it down effectively will win the most matches.

With a slower ball, the backhand overhead kill will be the shot of the future. I've never seen a pro use it consistently, but I know the shot can be hit because I've seen the racquet head speed developed in the backhand overhead smash in world class badminton. Fleming Dell, one of the world's top badminton players, hits his backhand overhead smash as hard as I can hit my forehand overhead smash. The power can be generated to hit an overhead kill or pass with the backhand, but it has not yet been developed in racquetball.

The Overhead Shots

There are actually three alternatives when the ball is waist-high or above: the defensive ceiling shot, the offensive overhead, or something in between that I call the Niederhoffer shot (after Victor Niederhoffer, the former top amateur squash player in the United States, who has also competed on the racquetball pro tour).

The ceiling ball is still the major defensive shot above the shoulder. With a medium-speed ball the ceiling shot is still an effective defensive tool. You will also have more room for error on your overhead kill if your opponent starts to hang back in anticipation of a ceiling ball.

Offensively, there is a wide arsenal of overhead shots, all of which can be hit with the backhand or the forehand. The flat overhead drive is probably the most versatile over-the-head shot. For the drive, you should contact the ball directly overhead and bring it down to the front wall somewhere between eighteen and twenty-four inches above the floor. The object is to hit the ball hard enough and high enough to drive your opponent into deep court but not to let the ball come off the back wall for a setup. The overhead drive is designed to force a weak return from your opponent. This is probably the best shot to learn first.

The most offensive above-the-waist shot is the overhead kill into the corners. The intent of the kill is to end the rally. It is most effective when you catch your opponent hanging back. Then you can fake as though you're going to the ceiling but flick your wrist downward instead, with just enough velocity to pop the ball into the corner.

One of my favorite variations of the overhead is the three-quarters-high slash, which is hit approximately shoulder-high with almost a roundhouse swing. The head of the racquet comes over the hand just as in a high overhead, except that the ball is hit at shoulder height. You can also drive the ball and kill to the corners. The slash is probably the easiest shoulder-high shot for beginners to hit consistently, and yet it is one of the hardest shots for the advanced player to perfect.

The Setup

The Upward Swing

The Backswing

The third above-the-waist alternative is the Niederhoffer shoulder-high pass shot. This shot is neither offensive nor defensive. In fact it looks like a nothing ball. It is hit neither hard nor soft. The shot may look harmless, but don't be deceived; it's one of the most difficult shots to return offensively.

When your opponents see you hit this shoulder-high nothing ball right to them, they can't believe their luck. Consequently, they continually leave the ball up in front court, which gives the easy finishing touch for Niederhoffer.

The Ceiling Ball Set up for the ceiling ball by positioning your feet and body toward the side wall, contacting the ball as low as possible, and angling it toward the ceiling. I get the most control and consistency if I start with my belly

The Forward Swing

Ball Contact

The Follow-Through

button pointing to the back wall. The ball should hit the ceiling between one and five feet away from the front wall, depending on the speed of the ball.

Another way to keep a fast ceiling ball from coming off the back wall is the hypotenuse theory: the farther the ball has to travel, the less velocity it will have. According to this theory, if you hit the ceiling ball from the deep left corner, for instance, you should angle your return into the center of the court so that it rebounds high into the deep right corner. However, just watch out for your opponent's smash!

Many years ago I used to put topspin on the ceiling ball, hitting it as hard as I could just to get it to deep court. Theoretically, to keep the fast ceiling ball from coming off the back wall you should use overspin, but this is very, very difficult to execute. Instead, I recommend hitting very lightly so you force your opponent, rather than yourself, to hit defensively. Then you should take the offensive.

The Overhead Stroke   The stance on the overhead is very similar to the stance on the ceiling ball. With your body parallel to the side wall, reach for the ball and contact it at the highest point possible. The stroke is almost like swatting a fly on the ceiling.

However, the proper point of contact is debatable. Carl Loveday, my coach and a former world class badminton player, believes that execution and timing are the critical factors. Therefore, he advocates hitting the ceiling shot when the ball is slightly behind the head, the overhead drive when the ball is directly above, and the overhead kill when the ball is slightly out in front, so that the inclination of the racquet face is pointing toward the direction you want the ball to travel.

I agree that this is easier to learn initially, but you should advance to hitting all three shots from the same spot. I feel that the angle of the overhead is such that it has to be hit too precisely not to hop up at all. So if you want to hit with some level of safety—that is, if you want to go two feet to a foot and a half into the corner and still win—then you have to get your opponent leaning back. You can do this if you're using exactly the same motion for the ceiling ball, overhead drive, and kill, right up until the wrist snap. In other words, I don't think you gain enough in execution to give up deception.

Loveday uses a badminton type of stroke for his overhead, which is a shorter and more deceptive stroke. His theory is that you should hit the ball just hard enough to get it to the corner and die. Loveday uses just enough racquet head speed to pop the ball into the corner.

Hogan, on the other hand, smashes his overhead just the way he hits his tennis serve. Hogan can get away with his hard overhead smash because of the fast ball and slick glass courts. However, with a medium-speed ball on a normal court, neither a tennis smash nor a slice is as effective as the other two methods—namely Loveday's badminton style and the side-arm slash—because power tends to pop the ball up higher for an easy return.

While most former tennis players tend to hit the tennis overhead and former badminton players tend to hit the badminton overhead, the three-quarter-speed side-arm slash is the only style unique to racquetball. The slash is probably the best style of overhead stroke for the general player.

Watch the Ball

The most important fundamental on overhead strokes is to watch the ball. If you fail to keep your eyes on the ball, your overhead will generally be mis-hit and go too low. Many players take their eyes off the ball and look to the corner they're aiming for.

To correct this problem, concentrate on watching the spot where the ball is contacted until the racquet has moved through the area. Then your head can drop to see the destination of your shot.

You should also concentrate on using a looping motion to generate racquet head speed. The loop is most useful on the overhead drive. It's hit just like all the pictures you've seen of Roscoe Tanner or Pancho Gonzalez hitting the tennis overhead.

Most tennis beginners are taught to hit the overhead just like hitting the head of a nail with a hammer—straight back, straight through. This is as primitive as the old swing in racquetball. If you can't time the loop at first, try swinging straight back and straight forward until you get the feel of contacting the ball with eyes raised and head erect. Practice popping through the ball with your wrist and let the racquet head guide the ball down to the appropriate height.

Remember that the forehand loop is similar to throwing a ball and the backhand loop is an uncoiling motion similar to throwing a Frisbee. The two actions are actually mirror images of each other.

Practice your overhead on both sides by hitting shallow ceiling balls to yourself. Point to the ball with your opposite hand or elbow while you get your racquet cocked behind your head. Throw the racquet head (like a Frisbee or ball, depending on whether the shot is backhand or forehand) at the ball and swivel your hips life a golfer.

Remember that the overhead, particularly the backhand overhead, is the shot of the future. If you begin mastering these techniques, you'll be one step ahead of the competition, unless, of course, they're practicing the overhead, too.

The New Strategies of Racquetball

Racquetball nowadays is primarily an execution game. It's no longer an all-out retrieving game where a player simply tries to get the ball back to the front wall to keep it in play, as in squash. Modern racquetballers play as close to the front wall as possible for accuracy—but still get a viable shot at every ball so that they can execute the winners.

The problem with staying in center court—the center-court theory (Fig. 1)—is that when a power player like Marty Hogan hits the ball and goes for a kill, it can't be covered.

So if you adopt the classic center-court theory, a powerful player is able to control the rallies and stroll around the court while you are running or diving yourself into the ground. This is the case even with pro players. No one is quick enough to stay effectively in the old center-court position.

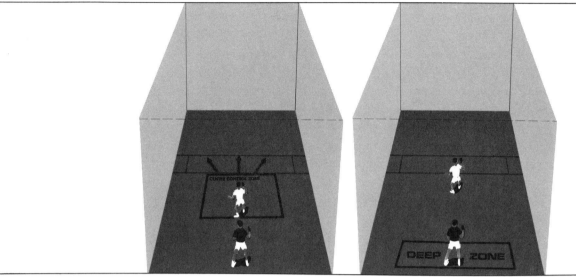

Fig. 1 The Center-Court Theory   Fig. 2 The Deep Zone

The Deep Zone I feel that nowadays the control zone has moved back to the point where it is worthless to call it center court. It is almost a deep back-court zone in the general area where you normally receive serve. Let me explain why.

There are two types of players, the attackers and the waiters. The attacker gets up front and cuts off the ball at the earliest opportunity. The attacker thinks that the sooner he cuts off the ball the less time the opponent has to react. The attacker requires catlike reflexes, acute vision, and a lot of luck. I think the attacker is becoming less effective in pro racquetball, where the waiter—and Marty Hogan is a prime example—will play deep court, wait for the ball, and hit it at the last possible moment. This strategy can work in amateur play, too.

The key to playing the deep zone (Fig. 2) is to flow forward as your opponent hits the ball. I believe that coming from a deep position and moving on the ball is a far superior strategy to that of the attacker. The attacker cannot move as gracefully or efficiently as someone coming from the back court who can move onto the ball, ready to hit it hard every time.

The best waiters and hitters from the deep zone come into the rally with the intention of ending it there and then. Hogan never comes to the ball with the thought of keeping it in play; he is out to execute a kill, and even if he doesn't succeed every time his mental attitude is probably going to win the game for him.

The Moving-Pocket Defense

What's a good defense against a powerful hitter? I recommend the moving-pocket defense. This is simply restricting the amount of court you must cover.

A racquetball court is just too big to cover adequately for every shot to any position. When I am play-

Fig. 3 Eliminate the Down-the-Line

ing, I eliminate certain shots from my cover. For example, I ignore the down-the-line shots (Fig. 3). Virtually no one can hit down the line with consistency without having the ball pop off the side wall or carry off the back wall, which gives the opponent plenty of time to cover wherever he happens to be on the court.

So I first eliminate the down-the-line alley, a lane about three feet wide stretching from front to back court. This decreases the amount of court I have to cover.

Now I can concentrate on covering the crosscourt shots, because during a normal match 75 percent of all shots go to a crosscourt coverage pattern either by a pinch or by the crosscourt drive. When a player rushes a shot, which happens under pressure, the tendency is to go crosscourt. When a player is late on a ball, which often happens when he's being beaten, he will invariably go side wall–front wall.

By eliminating the down-the-line, I reduce the a-mount of running I have to do and I can put myself in

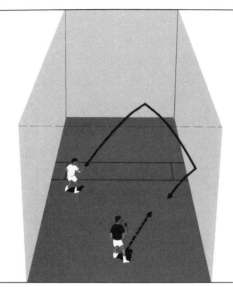

Fig. 4 Flow Down Upon the Ball

the position where I am flowing down on the ball almost 90 percent of the time.

Work out where the ball is going to go, move down on it (Fig. 4), timing your arrival—with your racquet ready—with the ball, and proceed to hit through it. The power of that play will have your opponent scrambling. Most players in front court can only scoop the ball toward the front wall; there just isn't enough time to set up with a good swing. Hogan always seems to have all the time in the world to hit shots, because he waits for the ball until the last possible moment. He almost looks like he's in slow motion.

So come forward, flowing on to the ball, and try to hit on arrival rather than panicking and reaching forward and flicking or popping the ball into the air.

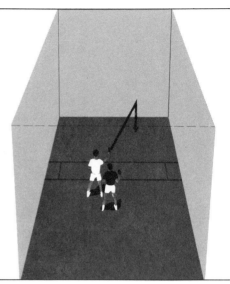

Fig. 5 Dictate by Position

**The Random
Combination** I feel that the ideal form of play is a random combination of selective coverage from deep zone plus an early intercept, because that will keep your opponent completely off balance. For example, for two points you might intercept early in the ball's passage; and for the next two points wait for it, powering it around the court to keep your opponent out of the flow. To do this, you must anticipate the ball's direction.

You can anticipate what your opponent is going to do and you can move your body to make your follow-up shot as easy as possible. We know that three out of four shots will go crosscourt, for example. Here are my keys to good anticipation:

1. Dictate by position. Your position can force the play. For example, you might stand close to your opponent so he will know you're covering for the down-the-line pass (Fig. 5). By making the situation look like he will have a hard time getting a down-the-line past you, you can force him to go crosscourt, which is exactly what you want.

2. *Prepare for the Sunday shot.* Every player has a Sunday shot—his favorite shot, one that he is confident in executing. Under pressure, you can be certain that your opponent will go for his Sunday shot. Know what it is and cover for it. In a lot of cases your shot-making can dictate the Sunday shot and you can react accordingly. Remember, the key is not to get to the ball, it is to get to the ball ready to hit.

3. *Analyze the swing.* It's easy even for a beginner. Normally if the ball is out in front of a player he will tend to go crosscourt. If the ball is behind him he will tend to go side wall–front wall.

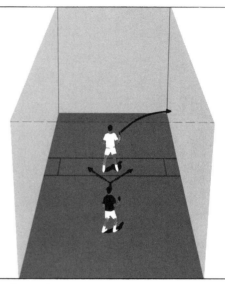

Fig. 6 Gamble on the Crosscourt

Defensive Situations What should you do when your opponent has an absolute setup? You've been in this situation. You've hit a mediocre-to-lousy shot and your opponent's in perfect position. He's got two seconds to hit the ball. Now what? You have three basic alternatives:

1. Take center-court position and wait and see. This is the least effective of all counters to a setup, yet it's the most used. Many players believe that if they are in center court they will have the best chance to cover the ball. Now, that's just not true on the absolute setup. On the absolute setup, the percentage play is to gamble to get back into the point, not to sit in center court and wait. I prefer the other two alternatives.

2. Gamble on the crosscourt. If my opponent has the setup from midcourt or closer, I'll try to come in behind him, and at the last second I gamble one way or the other (Fig. 6), depending on the three factors in anticipation I described earlier. Usually I'll gamble on crosscourt, because 75 percent of all balls go crosscourt. I will only change that if I feel that his favorite shot is usually other than crosscourt. I believe you should cover 75 percent of all balls well and the others hardly at all. That way you'll gamble, but you'll be much more effective in the long run.

3. *Fake your cover.* If the player is hitting from behind you, show him one look and then reverse your position. For instance, if your opponent has a forehand and is on the right side of the court, hitting down the right line, display a look as though you're gambling to cover the right corner and then, just as he swings, move to the left. Your opponent is probably thinking, "This guy's covering the right corner. I'll fool him and go to the left," which is exactly where you'll be waiting. So what you've done is dictate the shot.

Fig. 7 Back Against the Wall

How to Return a Serve

Many of the preceding principles also apply to the return of serve. The server has much the same advantage as the player who has the setup. But rather than waiting like a sitting duck for the server to dictate and dominate the play, I believe you should go for the percentages.

There are two positions for the serve return that are now being used by the pros. There's the Hogan I-don't-care-where-you-serve attitude, with your back against the back wall (Fig. 7), saying "I can execute so well that if you leave it up an inch I'll kill it." Then there's the Strandemo method, where the player is five or six feet from the back wall, hunched over, with his legs spread in a linebacker position, saying "Boy, am I going to hustle on this play." Neither of these positions is the best way to cover the ball. Only Hogan can get away with his method, while Strandemo feels he can move faster from a wide stance, standing up, than you can flowing in. That goes against the flow theory.

Fig. 8 Gamble on the Backhand

The server is going to drop the ball and serve it regardless of your flow, so I think it's best to gamble one way or the other. Since perhaps 90 percent of all serves go to the backhand side, you should move to the left a few times (Fig. 8). In fact, I'll go all the way to the left before the server even hits the ball, just to make him think twice and catch him off guard.

It's probably better to get aced a couple of times when you misguess the serve than to stay in center court and return none of the serves effectively. Remember that you can't cover the whole court. If you try to play a straight-up defense against a great server, you're going to be forever late on every serve, which is a great disadvantage. If you gamble and your guess is correct, you have a very good chance of ending the rally to your advantage because the server is generally off balance momentarily as a result of the big effort put into generating his or her power serves low and hard.

Crowding and Coverage Crowding can have an enormous effect on your coverage. For example, let's assume your opponent has a shot from somewhere near the middle of the court. Now, you can try to get as close to him as possible to move up to the front wall or you can move to where you think the shot's going to go.

The alternative to crowding an opponent is flowing in behind him and cutting in at the last moment. I believe in the flow-and-cut-in method. That gives you more balance and poses less chance of being hit by the racquet. It's also better sportsmanship.

Crowding is a trade-off between irritating your opponent by being near him, and flowing in from behind where you don't really bother him except that you're already on the move and he won't know which way you're going to gamble. I believe the second method really causes more confusion and less injury.

Game Plans for the Better Player

A game plan is an analytic, systematized method of attacking a certain game style. If you watch closely while a potential opponent plays, you'll realize that the shots made in certain situations become very predictable. Every player has a different style, but within that style he is usually pretty consistent.

For example, if you're playing someone who has a strong forehand and likes to shoot, you know what to expect when you give him a setup to the forehand. On the other hand you may realize that when given a setup to the backhand this same opponent always goes defensive. By being aware of this ahead of time you'll be one step ahead.

I recommend that you sit down with your coach, or a player you respect, and map out your game plan on paper. For example, before a match I diagram four or five serves that I want to concentrate on. I also make a list of dos and don'ts against that particular opponent. I even map out specific situations that are likely to occur, so that there will be fewer surprises for me during the match. If you've already thought your game plan through ahead of time, all you have to do during the match is execute.

Game Plan Rules Basically there are two rules for devising a game plan. Rule number one: Play your own game. Rule number two: Use a game style that forces your opponent out of his game style. Ideally, you should master a number of different styles so that you can always play your own game, but at the same time you'll be forcing your opponent out of his game style.

For example, if you're playing a power player like Marty Hogan and you're also a power player, you will lose to Hogan because you're letting him do what he does best. If you were a more versatile player, you would realize that you would be better off playing a slow, garbage game, keeping the ball high enough so that Hogan couldn't generate his tremendous power. However, if by switching to the slow, garbage game you actually do yourself more harm than good because the only style you can play is power, then stick to your game.

The greatest players in the history of individual sports have been the ones who mastered a variety of styles. During the course of your development as a racquetball player I suggest that you take the time to develop alternate styles. That way your game plan will cover all situations and you will find that few opponents give you any trouble. Good players can handle certain opponents but will be thrown off by others. Great players can handle them all.

Let's first look at the so-called pro style of play, which of course includes the style of Marty Hogan, the premier player in racquetball today. Hogan typifies what I call the bull, the supreme power player.

How do you confront the bull? Remember that there are areas in every power player's game where he can't hit with power. Those are the areas to aim for.

The musculature of the typical bull does not allow him or her to make a tight swing when reaching for high backhand shots. Marty Hogan is the exception to this, which is why he is so unusually deadly. But most bulls cannot hit hard high backhands, so aim for that region.

You should also try to move the bull out of his or her natural habitat. You want to move the bull into an alien position where he or she is forced to play pitty-pat racquetball, which may be more to your style of play. If there is an area where the bull can't hit the ball hard, keep the ball there the majority of the time and you'll tend to frustrate your opponent.

If, on the other hand, you run into a bull who seems to have no weak area to aim to, then at least hit away from the area where he hits the ball hardest. One method is to keep the ball as high as possible without having the ball carom off the back wall. You'll find that power players, no matter what their ability to hit with power, have a more difficult time killing from a higher angle. From that height the bull's power tends to work negatively because the ball will hit the front wall at such an acute angle that it pops up and gives you a chance to recover it.

Defending Against the Bull The shots you can use to keep the ball above the waist to prevent the bull from hitting with full force are the ceiling ball, the lob shot, and the garbage ball. I was probably the strongest all-time advocate of the ceiling ball. I was able to keep power players at bay by keeping any ceiling ball deep within two or three feet of the back wall at chest height. Because this is above the optimum power zone, the bull has problems trying to use power effectively against a well-placed ceiling ball.

The lob shot goes back in history to when the balls were considerably slower, so today we virtually have to remove the lob from our game plan, except as a desperation attempt when we have no other swing at the ball. Only in that case should you hit the lob shot to the bull.

The garbage ball is a five-foot-high, medium-speed pass shot that's designed to go either crosscourt or down the line. The modern leading advocate of the garbage pass is the squash champion, Victor Nieder-

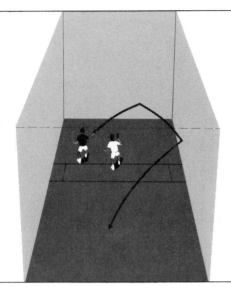

Fig. 1 The Bull: Hit Outside the Power Zone

hoffer. Vic's medium speed pass is frustratingly and tantalizingly high as it passes, yet the ball slows down as it catches the side wall or before it has a chance to carom off the back wall.

Another method of playing against the bull is to hit the ball outside the power zone. Most power players have to be able to extend the arm and hit through the ball with the entire body to generate power. You'll find that there are really two ways of keeping the ball out of the power zone. One is to hit the ball in such a way that it is beyond the swinging reach of the power player. This is normally done by the wide-angle pass.

The wide-angle pass (Fig. 1) is designed to hit the side wall slightly behind your opponent and carry in behind, dying as it reaches the back wall. This shot is very often combined with the Niederhoffer garbage trajectory, where the ball is hit high. Even if your opponent does try to cut the ball off prior to the time it reaches the side wall, it is really too high to do any-

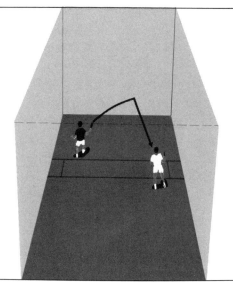
Fig. 2 The Bull: Jam the Player

thing with it without running into the acute-angle pop-up problem. However, you must hit this shot with plenty of touch or else the bull will either be able to cut it off or get a setup off the back wall (Fig. 2).

An alternate method of keeping the ball outside of your opponent's power zone is to keep it inside the zone. In other words, jam the bull. Hit the ball right at him.

A final method to include in your game plan against the bull is to slow the game down. Slow not only the pace of the game but the pace of your shot. The bull likes to play a jet-powered, slambang game in order to overpower. Instead, give him something off-speed so that he has to time it in order to hit hard. Make him supply his own power.

To slow down the pace of the game, try taking your time before putting the ball in play. Think about your shot before you hit it. Try to play the type of game that's going to make your opponent antsy. When the bull gets antsy, he will overswing when finally getting to the ball, so it carries off the back wall or else skips directly into the floor and bounces almost to the ceiling.

Now let's talk about playing the retriever, or the rabbit. This player usually doesn't have a lot of shots. The rabbit usually sets you up for what appears to be an easy shot with an open lane to hit into. You try to blow it by the rabbit and then he steps smartly over and rekills the shot!

Playing the Retriever

The rabbit loves to run. He loves to be in an off-balance position where he has to chase down the ball. Rabbits like to feel they're contributing to the match by giving it their all. A rabbit often tends to take a position well out of center court, because he is generally not a shotmaker. Generally, rabbits are in poor posi-

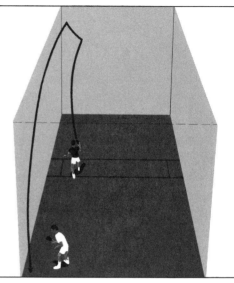

Fig. 3 The Rabbit: Go to the Ceiling

tion most of the time simply because they hit terrible shots.

In your game plan against a rabbit you should expect the rabbit to retrieve every ball. Never quit on the rally until the ball has bounced three times; even then, you still may not be able to quit.

Rabbits tend to hit most effectively on the run. They've been in that situation so much that they've gotten good at hitting while retrieving. On the other hand, what would be an easy kill to anyone else really throws off a rabbit's timing. The rabbit is not used to someone executing the ball so he doesn't have to run for it.

When I played a rabbit in the old days I almost exclusively went to the ceiling. That way the rabbit was stuck in the back corner (Fig. 3). No one was doing much running and it became a game of patience, intellect, and execution, at which, as a rule, the rabbit does not excel.

So you should hit the ball to the rabbit and you'll find he does less running and even less scoring. Don't attempt to play the rabbit's game, expecting the rabbit to tire, because rabbits can run forever and you'll probably be the first to drop.

The Shootist

The shootist is a shotmaker who usually lacks power but is constantly going for the bottom board. You can't be too careful against a player like that.

There are three ways I've found to beat the shootist. The first way to beat players who try to kill everything is to give them the worst possible percentage shot to shoot and then take good center-court position and cover. I know I've been critical of the traditional center-court theory, but against a shootist of only average power you can still play the traditional position.

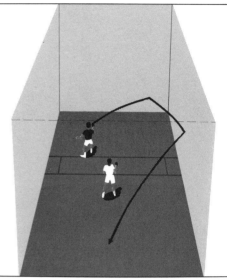

Fig. 4 The Shootist: Hit Away and Behind

When a shootist shoots the ball, he's looking to end the rally quickly. He may even try to win with a service return. If that is the case, you have the advantage of being in better position, since you will be in center court when you serve. From there you can anticipate the shot and start moving forward into the correct coverage zone much sooner.

Several shots will give the average shootist lots of trouble. For example, try the ceiling ball deep along the backhand wall or the overhead drive into the body. You might also hit the wide-angle pass (Fig. 4) away from and behind the shootist. If the shootist attempts to return any of these shots with a kill, the usual result is frustration. If, on the other hand, the shootist decides not to shoot and goes defensive instead, then you've forced him out of his game style.

Most people are weaker on their backhands, so when you play a shootist you should let him try to kill his backhand rather than the forehand. Figure out what shots you feel are the weakest in your opponent's repertoire, such as shots from deep court, and concentrate on them. If the shootist can roll the ball out from thirty-nine feet, he has earned the point. If the shootist skips the ball, you are given the point without even working. If the shootist leaves the ball up, then you should be ready to move in for the rekill.

The third way to handle a shootist, especially one who is deadly when killing the serve, is to try to serve more conservatively, rather than aggressively. Normally you can serve a decent low, hard drive and the average receiver is not going to try to shoot the ball. Chances are he will be off-balance and decide to go to the ceiling to be safe. However, when you're playing a high-percentage shootist who also has the ability to hit on the run, it's preferable to give him the most difficult shot to hit. Give him the high ball and make your opponent hit down with an acute angle so that the ball pops up.

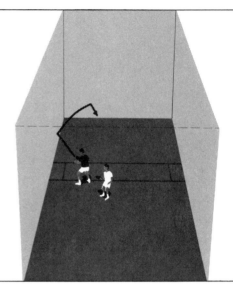

Fig. 5 The Crowder: Get Behind the Ball

The Crowder The crowder is the player who stays so close that he throws off the rhythm of your swing. However, most crowders will not get so close as to become subject to the waffle face, unless they have no regard for their own bodies. If you realize this, then all you need is complete mental discipline so you can play your own game and block out all distractions from your mind.

The second method of dealing with the crowder is to hit the ball so you are between the crowder and the ball (Fig. 5). That way, your body blocks the crowder's vision momentarily as you hit the ball, so his closeness has worked to his disadvantage. The crowder can't go around you and the referee can't call a hinder because the inopportune position is the crowder's own fault.

The third method of dealing with the crowder is the frontal attack with either racquet or ball. I don't recommend this in amateur racquetball, since your opponent usually is in the way only because he isn't aware of the proper position or has lost track of the ball.

Sportsmanship should be paramount in amateur play. If you feel there's any chance of hitting the other player with the racquet or the ball, you should hold up.

In pro tournaments, however, crowding is usually an intentional attempt to dictate which way your shots will go. If a player repeatedly does this after I've warned him and asked him as nicely as possible to move out of my way, I always hit the player as hard as I can in the back. If you do hit the crowder, do it somewhere that won't cause permanent damage but where you will cause audible pain.

The One-Armed Bandit

The one-armed bandit is the player who has a tough forehand but no backhand, or vice versa. Such players are usually to be found in the amateur ranks, but there are still a few among the professionals.

How do you play against people who can hit from only one side? Strangely enough, I think you should keep the ball to their strong side on the first shot. If you can do this and hit the ball well enough so that it is not killed, you'll have the whole court to hit to the weak side.

Naturally, every competitive racquetball player attempts to improve whatever weakness he has. But you'd be doing yourself a disservice if you hit every shot to an opponent's supposedly weak backhand. Eventually he will catch on and will be able to overcorrect his position to favor that side so he doesn't even have to move for the shot. In addition, if a player is forced to hit one particular stroke over and over again, he's bound to get sounder on that stroke, even in as short a time as the duration of a match.

So the best way to beat a one-armed bandit on the weak side is to force him to the strong side and then back to the weak side so that he or she has to play in

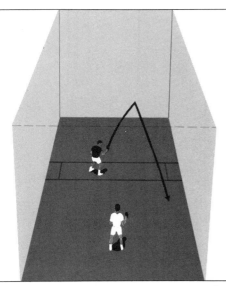

Fig. 6 The One-Armed Bandit: Hit to the Strong Side First

the center of the court without favoring either side. The one-armed bandit won't get enough work on the weak side to improve it, so you'll be able to exploit the one-sided weakness.

By serving occasionally to the one-armed bandit's strong side (Fig. 6) you'll probably catch him off guard enough for your serve to be an ace. Nothing is more demoralizing to the one-armed bandit than an ace to the strong arm, because if he loses confidence in that shot, there's nothing to fall back on.

The Dinker

What about the dinker? Playing against someone who hits the ball very softly can be a totally frustrating change of pace. The present power style of play, which most pros use and most amateurs aspire to, requires a constant, hard-hitting barrage of shots. But against the dinker your coverage patterns will be three or four feet closer to the front wall than usual, the ball will be traveling much slower than usual, and your timing will be completely off. It's no wonder that playing a dinker is often frustrating.

Probably the best way to foil the dinker is to play your own game. The mistake I used to make with dinkers was to try to outdink them. Do not dink with the dinker.

Neither should you try to overpower the dinker. All the dinker has to do against a power player is block the ball with a square racquet face to dump the ball in the corner. The dinker will try to use the power of your shot against you, so your best move is to hit a normal speed shot and force the dinker to generate the power.

Many of the shots you should use against a dinker are the same as you would use against the shootist. Shoot the ball before the dinker gets a chance to throw you off-balance. Give the dinker the low-percentage

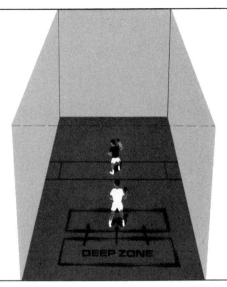

DEEP ZONE

Fig. 7 The Dinker: Move Your Zone of Defense Up

shots to shoot. Serve conservatively, rather than aggressively, against the dinker.

The shootist usually hits the ball with enough power so you can position yourself in center court and anticipate the kill attempt. The dinker, on the other hand, hits so softly that you have to move your pocket of defense up three or four feet to compensate for the shorter rebound off the front wall (Fig. 7).

The Turtle

Now let's examine the turtle, the player who is a slow mover but a good shooter. Most turtles are overweight and in relatively poor condition. They can't hit the ball on the run because they can't run. So simply reverse the principles you would use against the rabbit. On the serve, make the turtle lunge for the ball. Once you have

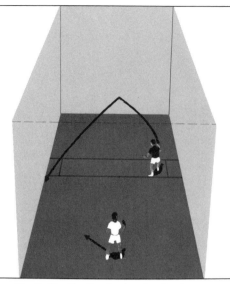

Fig. 8 The Turtle: Go for the Crack

the turtle on one side of the court, he will have a tough time recovering to the other side.

This is what I call the one-two punch of racquetball. Serve to the left, the turtle crawls over to the left and returns the serve, then you punch the ball down the right wall. There's very little chance of error, so your punch shot can be just about any height as long as it angles along the wall.

There are many serves you can use to set the turtle up for the one-two. You can serve the slow drive one inch over the line, but wide. You can serve the short-angle crack (Fig. 8) and the drive and fly.

In rallying against the turtle, your objective should be to keep the ball in play. While the rabbit never tires of chasing down your passes, the turtle will drop dead after a few long rallies. Don't kill the ball or hit perfect passes, because the turtle is an expert at knowing which shots are gettable and which are not. You're not going to tire the turtle if he or she won't run for your shots. Hit shots that are just barely returnable or else just out of the turtle's reach so that an attempt will be made to run after them.

What if you're playing a "hot" player? When you meet **Game Plan** someone on a hot streak, try to relax and don't panic. **Tactics** I've found over the years that the best way to handle a hot player is to ride the hot streak out. Don't reject your game plan just because your opponent rolls out the first four balls.

    Rarely will anyone be able to maintain a hot streak for three-quarters or even half of a game. So if you run into somebody who's annihilating you and your game plan, don't give up. Give your plan a chance to work. Stick with it because you spent a lot of time formulating your strategy. Chances are that this player is temporarily playing over his head. Eventually he'll cool down and you can take over.

When you are on top, you should stick to your winning game plan, even if your intelligent opponent switches his tactics to try to counter your winning streak. Don't change your plan simply because your opponent does. He's been forced to make the change; you haven't. Of course, sometimes your opponent's changes in position or shot selection or tempo will turn the tide. Then you should consider a change in your strategy.

One strategy to foil your opponent's game plan is to apply a little reverse psychology. For example, you might try to hide a weakness by convincing your opponent that it's your strength.

Sometimes it's better to gamble with your weakness early in the match. You might get lucky and roll the ball out so that your opponent will shy away from attempting that same shot against you. This is exactly what you want to happen.

If you try to play a safe-percentage game with your weakness, a better player will catch on and nail you into the ground. Of course, the reverse psychology won't work against someone who's played you before, so the best idea is to work at your game until you don't have any weaknesses.

8

How to
Win at Doubles

Communication is probably the single most important attribute of a solid doubles team. Ideally, you and your partner should communicate so well that you actually play as one. To approach this ideal, consider these four areas of communication:

1. Pregame communication. When I play an important doubles match, my partner and I always have a conference to discuss general coverage patterns, offensive tactics, and types of serves that we think will be particularly effective against our opponents. We try to anticipate what our opponents are likely to try against us and our possible moves. Once we've discussed these possibilities, our major decisions of general strategy are made and we're ready to play.

2. Communication during play. Before you play, decide on the verbal and hand signals you will use in play. The signals should be loud and clear, leaving no doubt as to what should be done. The player deeper in the court should call the signals, because he has a better view of the situation. "Mine!" "Yours!" "Switch!" and "Clear!" are the signals I suggest.

Team Communication

3. Communication during time-outs. Use your time-outs for communication or to stop your opponents' momentum. Time-outs or pauses between games should be used as a football quarterback would use the audible—to plan countermoves effective against unexpected maneuvers by your opponents.

4. Postgame communication. After each match you and your partner should review your performance. You might even keep a notebook on your matches. This will help you remember successful moves—and a few failures, too.

Keep Up Your Morale Your doubles team will be more effective if you can maintain the proper mental equilibrium. Cheer your partner on. Encourage him or her to go for bread-and-butter shots, and never, never criticize on the court.

If your partner is playing badly, handle this quietly and calmly during a time-out. Keep any criticism completely constructive. Your partner is just as sensitive and is trying just as hard as you are.

I also make it a point never to second-guess my partner by calling what could be his skips and double-bounce gets. We could argue the ethics of such a position all day. It is embarrassing for my partner to be staunchly defending his or her own shot or get and for me to side with the opponents. A "see no evil" approach is the best for team equilibrium.

Morale will be helped if you protect your partner on the court. For example, if your partner is stranded in the front court, hit a ball to the ceiling to give the poor guy an opportunity to move back to safety. Nothing is more discouraging than being caught in no-man's-land and having not only your two opponents, but your partner as well, blasting shots at you.

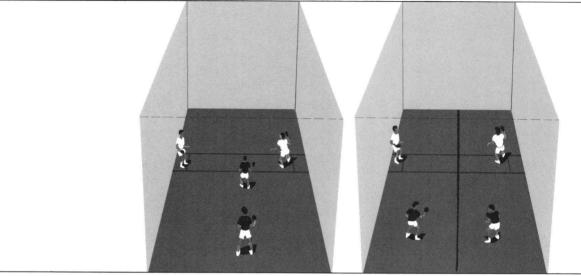

Fig. 1 The I Formation   Fig. 2 The Side-by-Side Formation

Doubles Formations
There are two common doubles formations—the I and the side-by-side. The I formation (Fig. 1) is the offensive/defensive alignment that places one team member up front to handle all the kill shot retrieving and rekilling while the other partner floats in the back court. The back-court player's responsibility is to return pass attempts and ceiling balls while also providing the long-range offense.

The advantage of the I formation is that it gives the better athlete, who should always be the back-court player, the free range and unbridled shot selection he needs to play his best. This can be a major disadvantage, too. The back-court player has to be big, strong, and extremely agile with a flawless back-court ceiling game.

The I formation can be attacked by four methods:

1. Move the back-court player until he is exhausted and you will have taken the edge off his offensive game.

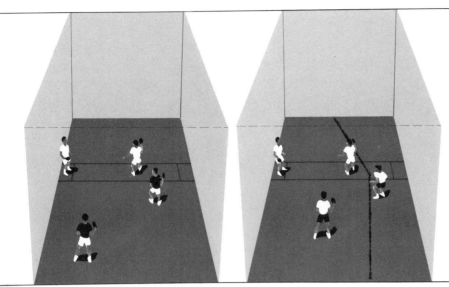

Fig. 3 The Diagonal Defense   Fig. 4 The Modified Diagonal Defense

2. Serve to the front-court coverer and shoot the first ball before he can rush into front court.

3. Kill the ball hard and low into the middle, leaving no chance for your opponents to make an effective return.

4. Use ceiling balls to force one player into the back left corner until he makes a weak return—then shoot whichever corner his partner has left uncovered.

The side-by-side formation (Fig. 2) should be the perfect arrangement. Side-by-side gives excellent coverage of the front court and lets each partner cover his or her own side.

However, side-by-side takes two ultraquick individuals using their forehands to keep power drives from getting by down-the-lines with no one deep to pick up the slack. A player using his backhand up that close would be pounded unmercifully by pure and wide V drives. The answer is the diagonal defense (Fig. 3).

The majority of doubles players are right-handed.

The I Formation

When a right-hander has to react to a fast shot, his tendency is not to go crosscourt. Thus, most hard drives in doubles go to the left side (crosscourt for a right-hander). A lefty rarely plays right side, so there is always a forehand over on the right side to cover the drives on that side. Consequently, the right-side player can play closer.

Thus, most doubles teams play a modified diagonal defensive (Fig. 4) that allows the left-side player to protect himself by playing back slightly yet leaves the right player to stay up to cover for most kill shots to the front right corner.

The Center-Court Theory The team that controls center court is the team that wins. When a team is caught in the back court, the front-court team can easily cover the kill shots. In dou-

The Side-by-Side Formation

bles most of the points are scored on kill shots, whereas in singles many points are scored on well-placed passing shots. Passing is not as effective in doubles, because two people can easily cover the two halves of the court.

When your team is up front, you can take greater advantage of those front-court plums. The team hitting ten or fifteen feet from the front wall will be more accurate than the team hitting from thirty-five to thirty-eight feet.

The front-court team has better visibility. Vision is extremely important in doubles, because the play is so quick. The team in the back court has to pick out the ball through the four legs and four arms of the team that's in the front-court position.

In an experienced doubles team, one partner often feels more comfortable and plays better in the front court. You can defeat this team by always serving to the front-court coverer. If the coverer has to return

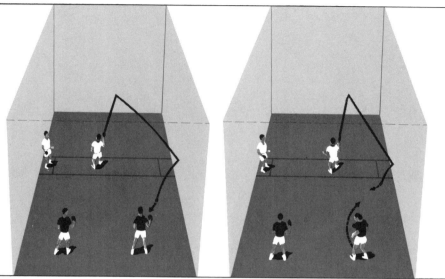

Fig. 5 Serve the Coverer   Fig. 6 Fly the Return of Serve

serve, then it will be much more difficult for him to move into the front court. This is especially true if your serve forces him to return from the very deep corner (Fig. 5) and is doubly effective if the serve is so good that it makes him lose his balance.

If the receiver makes a weak return, there may be no one up in front court to play defense and your team can score an easy point. If your opponents use this tactic against your team, you can

1. Hit a ceiling ball, which will give you, the coverer, time to move into the front court.

2. Take an aggressive service return position; that is, inch up in the court and try to fly the return of serve (Fig. 6).

3. Alert your partner to take an extra step into the center (Fig. 7) to close up the zone and give you protection so you can move up front later.

The other tactic for defeating the center-court theory is the isolation theory. If one of your opponents

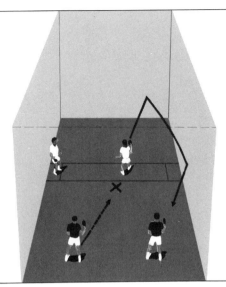

Fig. 7 Close the Zone

does not get to hit shots for long periods of time he will become rusty and cold. His timing will not be nearly as sharp when the time does come for him to hit the ball.

Eventually, the isolated player will become so desperate to hit the ball that he will have a tendency to poach into his partner's territory. This causes a breakdown in teamwork, because once poaching starts to occur no one will know who is going to take what. Also, morale slumps, because the impression is given that the poaching partner doesn't have complete confidence in his teammate.

On the other hand, the player hitting all the shots may start making his shot selection too aggressive and so will give up a number of easy points. That causes a complete decay of teamwork and morale as his disenchanted teammate jumps over to his side to help out.

The only effective defense against the isolation theory is to hit the ball so that it becomes very difficult to keep the ball in one particular area of the court. For example, use a medium-speed overhead drive rather than sticking completely to the ceiling ball. A ceiling ball rally is the easiest way of keeping the ball to one person. However, it takes tremendous poise to take a well-hit overhead drive coming into your body and do anything more than just hit it.

Doubles Combinations The lefty-righty combination has proven itself to be the best arrangement for winning doubles. Those two big forehands can be hit down their respective side walls. And a good player can often run around a shot directed down the middle and so get a forehand on it.

If lefty-righty is the best, what should you do if you're not fortunate enough to find a southpaw part-

Fig. 8 Drive Serve up the Middle

ner or if you and your partner are both lefties? Here are a few tactics that can be used to defeat the lefty-righty team:

Try to create a situation where both of your opponents go for the same ball. For example, hit most of your serves down the middle. Not only will this confuse the opposing team, but you're very likely to see a backhand used for return rather than the more powerful forehand.

Since most singles serves are designed to avoid the center, I suggest you consider these serves in doubles play:

1. *A low hard drive up the middle (Fig. 8).* Be careful to keep this serve very low, because if it comes off the back wall the opponent will have time to adjust to a forehand.

2. *The medium-angle Z.* This will confuse your opponents and, since it's a slowly developing serve, keep

your opponents a little deeper and out of center court longer.

3. *The low hard drive to the corner.* Hit this one deep so it dribbles around the corner toward the center. The receiving player won't know whether to back rapidly away to try and get a forehand on the ball, to spin around and hit a backhand, or to let the ball go all the way over to his teammate.

You can also try to confuse your opponents during the rally itself. For example, I aim my ceiling balls down the middle rather than try for a wall hugger down either the left or right walls. Not only does this force one of your opponents to backpedal rapidly to try to get in position to hit a forehand, but it also all but eliminates giving up those pesky setups that result when a ceiling ball catches a side wall too far toward the front wall.

Occasionally I'll try hitting a controlled drive from an overhand stroke designed to drive the ball down the

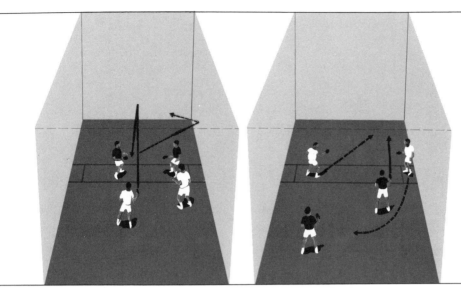

Fig. 9 The Fake

Fig. 10 The Front-Court Flood

middle with good pace and yet not come off the back wall. This is an excellent tactic and causes many mishit returns.

In addition to these defenses, there are a few special tricks of the trade that righty-righty teams can employ to score their doubles victories:

1. The fake. The setting for this maneuver is a slow ball hit down the right center of the court (Fig. 9). Player A moves over from his right side position and sets up to hit his backhand, yelling "I got it." The other player also sets up to take the ball with his forehand. This dual motion forms an arc of legs, bodies, and racquets that keeps both opponents deep in the court for fear of creating a backswing contact avoidable hinder. At the last second, player A drops his racquet and steps back away from the play and his partner slides in a right wall–front wall kill. Not surprisingly, no one gets within twenty feet of touching the ball.

2. The front-court flood (Fig. 10). This causes your

The Open Court Play

opponents to misread the actual coverage zones and squander precious setups. For example, if your right-side opponent gets a setup from half to three-quarters court and prepares to kill the ball in the right corner, you then leave the left side completely open and move into almost a front-court, I formation defensive position. The shotmaker has to think twice about shooting a ball with the defensive player that close to his target area and has a tendency to bypass the kill attempt and drive the ball crosscourt. Meanwhile, your partner can move over to the left to cover the crosscourt drive and hit the ball to the ceiling so the rally will start again.

3. *The open court.* With a strong partner you can stay close to the right and let your partner take all the setups out of the back right corner with his forehand (Fig. 11). While your partner moves back to a deep right, you should establish a position perhaps three feet from the right side wall—just enough room to allow your partner to shoot down the alley. If the right-side

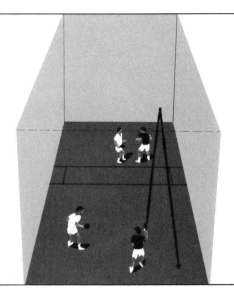

Fig. 11 The Open Court

opponent took a position to your left, your opponents could slide the ball for a kill exactly down the right wall. If your opponents attempt to cover the alley, your partner can pinch the ball off the right wall just in front of you. The opponents won't see a thing.

Playing the right side in a righty-righty combo requires much more patience than playing the left. Your primary responsibility is to position and to move in such a way as to discourage offensive shots in the right front corner. Try to force the play deep and over to the left side where your partner will have plenty of time to set up and work for a forehand offensive opportunity. The mortal sin of right-side play is sticking your backhand out and taking away your partner's forehand.

As a general rule, anytime you have to reach to the left for a backhand, your partner has time to make a better shot with his forehand.

Opponent Out of Position

Advanced Play   In doubles, movement of the offense and defense depends on the path of the serve. Ideally, both teams should move to their respective formations as soon as possible after the ball is served and returned.

For instance, if the serving team is playing a modified deep left diagonal, the left-side player should back out quickly two steps toward the back wall and at least a step and a reach from the left side wall. The right-side player should not move as deep in the court but should be careful to move quickly away from the side wall.

Although it's hard to generalize at the more advanced levels of play, here are six rules to keep in mind:

Rule 1. Follow every single swing of your opponent to your primary front-court coverage zone. This means playing without the ball and always being in motion.

Rule 2. If your opponent is forced out of position, automatically flow into a singles coverage pattern.

The Perfect Setup

Move back to your normal coverage position as you see your partner regain his proper shot.

Rule 3. Play closer from a serve return position and aggressively rally and follow in any weak return.

Rule 4. If the serve goes to your partner, forcing him deep, remember that you have to move temporarily into singles coverage, even if you are ordinarily the deeper player.

Rule 5. If the ball comes directly at you in front court and you have to make a quick decision on which way to jump, always move out of the way of the weaker shotmaker. This movement takes the stronger opponent away from the play.

Rule 6. If your partner has a setup from his side of the court, you should move as if you have to cover the shot. This will put you in an excellent singles coverage position if the rally continues, or if you're there first, your opponent will have to work harder for a good court position.

9

Have Fun
with Mixed Doubles

Mixed doubles is a game that requires some advanced instruction and careful forethought. Otherwise what should be a relaxed social activity can become a disorganized and potentially dangerous game.

First of all, I recommend becoming quite familiar with doubles positioning and strategy before even attempting a mixed-doubles match. You can learn about doubles by watching experienced teams, focusing your attention not on the ball but on the players individually and as teams.

It's particularly true in mixed doubles that both team members are never going to be identical in skill. I think this is even more apparent in open mixed-doubles tournaments, because only the top female pros can compete on the same level with a male player. So the stronger player—usually the man—will be in charge, developing strategy, calling time-outs, and taking the lead in communicating on the court.

Team Communication

Keep in Touch Constant communication is probably the single most important attribute of a solid mixed-doubles team. You and your doubles partner should always be talking—before the match, during the rally itself, during time-outs, and between games—and reviewing after the match. During the rally keep your signals short and sweet, such as "Yours!" "Mine!" "Switch!" and "Clear!" You might even try to come up with hand signals to telegraph which serve you're going to hit.

Part of the fun of mixed doubles is the camaraderie of the sport. In any team competition communication and morale maintenance are crucial. But all communication should be positive. Be sure that any criticism is constructive and given only during the privacy of a time-out or briefly between rallies. As partners you must keep up morale. Much of your success in racquetball depends on mental attitude and concentration—so cheer each other on!

Stronger Player on the Left

If both partners are right-handed, the stronger player should play the left side, for two reasons. First, the left-side player will cover more of the court, because his forehand will be toward center court. The left-side player covers all the balls on the left wall and the center while the right-side player returns the balls mainly on the right side. Weaker singles players can often play well in doubles, because their backhands are virtually unnecessary when they play on the right side.

Secondly, the stronger player is more effective on the left side because most players are used to hitting everything to the left side. This is a carry-over from singles play against a right-hander, whose backhand would be on the left side.

The most basic doubles strategy—the isolation theory—encourages ganging up on the weaker player. The usual result is that the weaker player becomes exhausted while the stronger player is tempted to poach (taking shots that the partner would ordinarily return). Then the teamwork breaks down and the game deteriorates.

As long as the weaker player is positioned on the right side, it will be more difficult for the opposing team to recondition its thinking and hit everything down the right. This is similar to the problems encountered when playing a lefty in singles.

The isolation theory also succeeds in cooling off the stronger player, who sees very little action in the game and will probably overreact when the ball finally does end up on his half of the court.

The Formations Partners also must decide who plays front and who plays deep. The I formation puts one player in front court ready to rekill anything that doesn't roll out. The player in deep court is there as a backup for anything that gets by the front-court player.

If you're playing a team that's using the I formation, you can defend in four ways:

1. Move the person in back court from side to side until exhaustion sets in.

2. Serve to the person who usually covers up front and then kill the next ball before he gets a chance to move up.

3. Kill the ball low and hard up the middle. The front-court player will probably not react in time and it will be too late for the back-court player to move up.

4. Hit ceiling balls to the back left corner and wait for a weak return. Then shoot to whichever corner is least guarded by the offensive partner in front court.

The Diagonal Defense

An alternative to the I formation is the side-by-side grouping. The problem with this arrangement is that if one partner moves in to pick up a kill, the opponents are sure to deal a powerful pass to that side.

The best of the I and the side-by-side formations can be combined in the diagonal defense. Divide the court in half diagonally, usually from the front left corner to the back right corner. The reason for using this direction and not the opposite is that most people are right-handed. Thus, the left-side player will be hitting backhands most of the time. Since few people have stronger backhands than forehands, the left-side player will be more effective playing deep, where he has more time to react and get the backhand around to the left. The player on the right can react more quickly and play more offensively into the front right corner. There isn't much defense against the diagonal, which is why I recommend it.

The truly macho types often play the J formation, named for its infamous proponent, Jay Jones. This player positions his partner in the back right corner, while he covers the entire court by himself. Not only is this unfair to the poor woman, but it's unsportsmanlike to everyone and can be dangerous. To be the ultimate poacher and apply the J formation takes tremendous stamina. It's like playing one against three because the partner becomes another obstacle rather than part of the team. It also takes a lot of gall. Don't do it.

Beating the J formation depends on how good the court hogger is. Unfortunately, the court is small enough so that a better-than-average player can cover it quite well alone most of the time. About the only thing you can do is attack the hogger's side in critical areas of the court—the corners.

Protect Your Partner In mixed doubles you must each protect your partner. Two cases come to mind immediately. First, if your partner makes a great get up in front court, be considerate enough to get the ball to the ceiling at the first opportunity so your partner will have time to return to proper position. Don't get caught in no-man's-land where not only your two opponents but also your partner may be whizzing shots by your head.

Secondly, do not hit hard-drive serves directly behind your partner, almost guaranteeing that she or he will be hit by the service return. It's fine to lob to that side of the court, because with the five-foot safety rule your partner will have enough time to decide whether to jump out in center court if the serve stays on the

Protect Your Partner

wall, or to stay in the box if the serve hits the side wall and angles into the center. Even in this latter case you should still get into center court as quickly as possible.

Play the Center

Mixed doubles is more enjoyable with the slower ball so that everyone has time to react and be in a safe position on the court. This safety zone, where you or your partner should be most of the time, is center court. The only time during the rally when you should leave the center court is when you are taking a shot or when the ball is behind you in center court.

For someone who has never played mixed doubles it's a little intimidating to be packed into center court with two other players. In intense moments, particularly with aggressive players, there can be some el-

Center-Court Control

bowing and feet getting stepped on in center court—especially in matches without officials.

But it's the team that controls center court that usually wins the game. Therefore you should take most shots on the fly, rather than letting them go to the back wall. If you wait to hit the ball off the back wall you are taking yourself out of center court, shooting from a greater distance to the front wall, and giving your opponents more time to react and reposition themselves in center court.

It is also important to position yourself in center court to allow your partner to hit crosscourt passes. Nothing is more embarrassing to you, or frustrating to your partner, than being hit by your partner's perfect pass shot because you are out of position. It's also a matter of safety. If you get between your opponent and the ball—watch out!

Make Mixed Fun!

Even in practice games I usually stress the importance of trying to win. This is for your ego as well as for getting used to maintaining a high level of intensity any time you step on the court. But I think mixed doubles should be the exception. If your only concern is winning at all costs, mixed doubles will no longer be a fun, social sport, which is what it's intended to be. Winning is a nice by-product, but it shouldn't be your sole objective if all four players are going to have a good time and leave the court on good terms, with their bodies still intact.

In racquetball, most women just can't compete with men on an even scale. I'm convinced that men are definitely quicker with their hands and feet.

So it's only fair to require that the man serve to the man and the woman serve to the woman to equalize the competition. Otherwise the men will try to take advantage of the women. You might also experiment with alternating hits as in table tennis, though I'm afraid this would end up in the man's getting the point every time he hit to the woman.

Men should watch out so they don't spend their time directing and becoming the puppetmaster—getting so involved in directing their partners that they end up not watching the ball. I remember when my wife, Pat, and I were playing mixed doubles against Ron Starkman and Ann Delaney. While Ron was busy telling Ann to get out of the box as he served, the lob he'd just served came down and hit him on the head.

Pat and I have attempted to play mixed doubles on a few occasions. But it's especially difficult to play with your spouse. We call this situation divorce court. Women who participate in mixed doubles should be ready to take on the responsibility for their half of the court—to do their share. If a woman is too timid and dependent on her partner, he's likely to resort to the J formation!

10

Practice for Perfect Play

Few racquetballers give much thought to organizing practice sessions to perfect their game. Practice sessions should involve a lot more than merely hitting the ball around by yourself while you're waiting for your partner to suit up.

It's essential to work toward a goal with your practice. But in order to work toward a goal, you have to define that goal. This can best be done with the aid of your local teaching pro. He or she should be able to work with you on the basic strokes and help you decide what style of play fits your personality.

Another excellent way to decide what kind of player you want to become is by watching the pros or the top-level amateurs in your area. If you have a fiery, temperamental personality, you are probably more comfortable playing an aggressive, banging style of play. At the other extreme is the laid-back, overanalytical person who spends time philosophizing about the game but rarely puts his or her theories into practice. If the overanalyzer ever does step on court, you can be sure that player will have a defensive, percentage style of play.

Use a Chart The analytical player often uses paper and pencil to chart improvement and projected goals. This is something that all players should do.

When I go out on the court, I identify six major areas of the court: zones one and two—left and right front court; zones three and four—left and right center court; and zones five and six—left and right back court. I then choose three shots to each zone; for example, straight kill, pinch, and wide-angle V kill to zone one. You should pick three shots you feel comfortable with for each zone.

By practicing three shots from each area you will have a complete repertoire of alternative coverage patterns. Once you practice your eighteen different shots (three times the six areas you hit from) to the point that they become repetitive and natural, you will be able to keep your opponent guessing during a match, without demanding any improvising on your part during the rally. By limiting yourself in this way, you can become proficient at a number of often-used shots that become automatic during the match.

When I used to practice ceiling balls, I'd hit a thousand ceiling balls a day. I'd keep hitting them until I hit ten perfect wallpaper ceiling balls in a row. I feel that you should come up with a number to practice as a reference point, but you should continue only until you've achieved your goal. It's not how many shots you've hit but how many successful shots you've hit that counts.

Your chart is always going to be changing as you improve. After you've mastered the shots you've selected in practice, you'll need to work on them only enough to tune them up. After ceiling balls become second nature, you might try hitting five good ceiling balls and then—let's say—going for an overhead drive crosscourt.

Most of you reading this book are not going to put in that much effort, because racquetball is not your profession. It's your recreation, so you want to keep it fun and keep it in the right perspective in your life. You don't have all day to think about creativity on the racquetball court. But if you learn just three effective weapons from each of the six zones on the court, you're going to find that you're much more successful than if you try to hit something new every time.

As an analytical player you'll also chart your percentages for each shot practiced. This can be invaluable to see how far you've improved. It's also handy as a reference before tournament play. If you think you have the luxury to wait for a shot that you know you can make 90 percent of the time, then do so. But if you find that your opponent is too good to give you that luxury, then you might have to use your backup shots even though your percentages may be only 70 to 75 percent.

In my prime I hardly ever attempted a kill shot that I could not execute 80 percent of the time. The rest of the shots hit consisted of controlled passes and ceiling balls, so I could wait for an opportunity to hit the ball from a zone where I had been more successful in my practice sessions.

Practice Sessions How long should you practice? Practicing for more than an hour causes most people to lose the advantage of the practice. But you should practice for as long as you can keep the intensity. Even professionals do not practice as much as they should.

When I was younger I could keep my intensity longer than I do now; over the years my concentration and desire have decreased. Other older athletes tell me that they have had the same experience.

I have cut back my practice sessions drastically. I practice only three times a week, an hour at a time. When I was younger I would hit a couple thousand shots every day. Now I hit only a couple hundred, but I still chart the percentage that I hit well, so I can see the trends. I also use my chart book to record how well each shot held up in a game situation as compared to the week before. That way I can see my improvement, and that's what's fun in the sport.

Visualize Your Strokes Visualization is important in all aspects of our lives. It goes along with positive thinking. If you can imagine yourself thin or rich or outgoing or quick or powerful, it's more likely that you will achieve your goal.

I've heard a lot of players remark on how much better they play after a long break. They seem amazed that, without spending any time on the court in months, their backhand, for example, is much stronger. But this doesn't surprise me at all, because what they probably have been doing in that time spent away from the court is thinking about their game a lot more.

Let's assume that you've watched enough players

to decide what type of player you are. Once you know whom you want to use as a model, watch that player—via live play, clinic demonstration, videotape, or televised tournaments—until you have a visual image of the player's stroke.

Once you can visualize the strokes, don't immediately go down to the court and play a game, hoping to incorporate the new image right away. First, practice in front of a mirror so that you can project your mental image onto the physical image you see reflected in the mirror. Work through the strokes patiently in front of the mirror until you can see yourself more or less corresponding to the mental image you have of the player you want to emulate.

Once you can swing your racquet in front of the mirror, memorize the feeling of it and try it with your eyes closed. Spend time in front of the mirror or off the court, making your body go through the stroke until your muscle memory takes over. Even if the new stroke seems funny or different at first, it will begin to feel normal to you after visualizing and practicing in front of the mirror. Pretty soon you won't be able to remember how you once hit the ball.

When to Practice

Most people have to practice when they get off work or out of school or work it around their family schedules. As a professional player I like to practice before I play and a little more after I play in addition to my regular practice sessions.

But the majority of you are amateurs and plan to

stay that way. So I think perhaps 20 percent of your time on the court should be spent practicing. Any more time than that would only take away from the cardiovascular and recreational aspects of the game—the major reasons why most people play.

When you practice, concentrate on only one element of your game at a time. For example, one day I might work on arm extension. The next day I might work on eye contact. The challenge of racquetball is that you can never run out of fundamentals to work on.

Always aim for a target. Just as having a goal focuses your mind, having a target focuses your effort during your practice sessions. You can use cans, tape on the walls, or tape on the floor. Some courts even have targets for various serves painted on the front wall.

By aiming for a target I am not suggesting that you look at the target while you're hitting the ball. That would bring your head up too soon and make you mishit. Always watch the ball, but be sure you know where you are aiming. Hearing the ball hit the can tells you you've hit the target. So use your mind to visualize the target and use your eyes to watch the ball.

Once you've mastered a certain angle or a particular stroking technique, you must brush it up occasionally, but you don't need to grind it into the ground. Once you've gained confidence through repetition in a certain area of your game, it's time to move on to something else.

You should find someone of approximately your own skill level who is interested in spending a half hour or so on the court, trying to improve. Having a practice partner is especially important for the two most important shots of the game—serve and return of serve. **Find a Practice Partner**

Practice by limiting your rallies to three shots. You serve, your partner hits a good return, and you then try to end the rally on the third shot. But even if you don't, stop the rally and start again with another serve. Then switch roles so that you can practice your serve returns and your partner can practice serves.

Now you're finally ready to practice during an actual game situation—one in which you're playing to win. How do you change from the relaxed practice session to the more intense practice game?

Sometimes it helps to bet on the game. Of course, some players require higher stakes to get fired up. Paul Haber, the greatest handball player of all time, would play games where he would allow himself only two swings once the ball was served. If he didn't win the rally by that time, the other player won the point. But Paul would be playing for a hundred dollars a point. That's one way to improve your intensity and concentration. However, unless you're as awesome as Haber was, betting might not do much to improve your personal financial situation.

One way to improve is by playing people better than yourself. This is invaluable on your way up the racquetball ladder. But just try to imagine the problems if everyone insisted on only playing people better than themselves. So in the name of fairness, if you're the best player in your area, you will have to play lesser-ranked players.

When this happens, think of it as doing a favor to

yourself. Playing someone below you in ability can actually improve your game if you know what to practice. Do this by restricting your game to force more pressure on one of your weaknesses so that it won't remain a weakness.

For example, I usually work on my backhand kill shot by telling myself that I can score only with my backhand, even though my natural game is to score with my forehand and play defensively with my backhand. So that puts additional pressure on my weaker stroke and evens out the competition.

Alternatively, I might allow myself to run only one point at a time. If I have the serve and then score a point, it's side out regardless. But my opponent gets to keep serving and scoring as long as he wins the rally. This puts added pressure on my serve returning. It's also unlikely that I can gather momentum, so I have to establish my own momentum on each shot. Or I may limit myself to one serve instead of the customary two attempts. This puts added pressure on me to get my first serve in since I don't get a second chance.

During game situations with weaker players you might also practice different playing styles. Sometimes I'll hit nothing but ceiling balls to warm up and see if I can get my opponent to make the mistakes. The second half of the game might be devoted to giving my opponent a tour of the court, hitting nothing but wide-angle passes and soft pinches. For the second game I might start off with a maintain-center-court-at-all-costs attitude by attacking everything and cutting off any passes before they get past me. Then to finish up the second game I might let every ball drop, wait patiently, and use the back wall as much as possible.

11

Get in Shape for Winning Racquetball

Racquetball is great for conditioning the heart, lungs, and circulation, but a serious player has to do more than just play in order to be able to be in top shape for a tournament.

Agility, strategy, flexibility, speed, and strength are required to improve. While the first two factors can be developed by playing the game itself, you should train off the court to develop flexibility, speed, and strength.

You can work on your heart and lungs by doing a series of exercises, most of which may be performed at home. Bicycling, running, wind sprints, and flexibility exercises will benefit your cardiovascular system and improve your footwork, balance, and court sense.

A superior racquetball conditioning program should take about two or three hours a week. Half of this time should be spent in strength conditioning, about one third on speed training, and the rest on flexibility exercises.

Arm Circles

Here's the conditioning routine I try to follow every week:

Monday: ten minutes of stretching exercises followed by thirty minutes of strength conditioning and twenty minutes of speed training (including warm-up and cool-down).

Tuesday: five minutes of stretching and fifty-five minutes of racquetball.

Wednesday: repeat of Monday's routine.

Thursday: repeat of Tuesday's routine.

Friday: repeat of Monday's routine.

Saturday: repeat of Tuesday's routine.

Sunday: swimming or relaxation.

Torso Twists

Crossleg Toe Touches

For flexibility and warm-up I recommend these exercises that you can do either on the court or at home:

Stretching Exercises

Arm circles—Gradually increase the size of the circles while increasing the speed.

Torso twists—ten to each side, twisting as far as your body will go.

Crossleg toe touches—Standing with your legs crossed, touch your toes ten times slowly.

Leg overs—Lie on your back on the floor with your arms stretched out to your sides. Lift your right leg over your body and try to touch your left hand. Hold for five seconds and release. Then do the same with the left leg over to the right hand. Repeat five times to each side.

Groin Stretch

Groin stretch—Stretch one leg out to the side and bend at the knee on the other leg. You will gradually be able to get lower and lower to the floor.

Achilles tendon stretch—Face the wall, standing a few feet away. Place your hands on the wall for balance while gently stretching one foot behind you. Try to get your heel flat against the floor so that you can feel the tendon stretching.

Jumping jacks—Start with twenty, but remember to keep your arms straight all the time.

Backward running—Once around the court if you can.

Side shuffle—Once around the court normally, once around with knees bent and hips low to the floor.

Skipping—Once around the court with the knees high.

Achilles Tendon Stretch   Jumping Jacks

For strength training in the gym or at your health spa: **Strength**
                                                            Training

1. Basic leg and back strengthening exercises:
Monster walks—Start with your feet together and lunge
out on your right foot. Then push off your right foot
and return to your original upright position.
Half squats—Use a vertical squat machine if available.
The angle formed with the upper and lower leg at the
bottom of the squat should be ninety degrees.
Heel raises—Also on vertical squat machine. (If you
don't have access to a machine, do a series of toe
raises.)
Single leg hops—Hop around the court on one foot.
Back hyperextensions—Use the Roman chair. Start

Side Twisting Sit-ups

with your hands behind your back. Place your hands behind your head for a more advanced exercise.

2. Exercises to improve strength for racquetball swing:

Side twisting sit-ups—Use a slant board and work up to a steeper angle.
Side hyperextensions—This is an advanced technique for well-conditioned athletes only. Work up to fifteen repetitions on each side.
Pullover torso machine—Find a weight with which you can perform no more than twelve repetitions.
Forehand arm swing—Use the high pulley station.

3. Exercises to improve general arm strength:

Triceps extensions—Use the high pulley station. Find a weight with which no more than twelve repetitions can be performed. Resistance should be increased weekly.

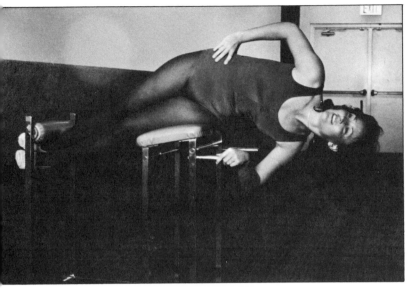
Side Hyperextensions

Exercise Bike

Alternate dumbbell curls—Find a weight with which no more than ten repetitions can be performed. Increase the resistance weekly.

Squats and push-ups—From a standing position, squat down with your hands on the floor in front of you, kick your legs out straight behind you, do one push-up, return to the squat, and then stand up again.

4. Exercises to improve your speed.

For speed and conditioning I recommend several exercises, but first warm up by walking or jogging slowly until you feel your body temperature rise.

Jogging or exercise bike—Begin with whatever you think you can handle. Gradually build up the distance and the pace. Six-minute miles are ideal for an advanced program, while some players may start out with two ten-minute miles and work up from there.

Wind sprints in sand—All sand training should be done

in intervals of twenty yards and at 90–100 percent effort for each interval. Because the effort will be maximal, be sure to warm up thoroughly prior to each training session.

Squat jumps—One leg forward, one leg back; one in the sand if possible. Do one set of twenty jumps at half effort, followed by two to five sets of twenty repetitions at full-out effort.

Bunny hops—Squat at one end of the court and hop to the other end as quickly as a jackrabbit. Race your doubles partner.

Barrel race—Place six Frisbees or similar objects in a straight line, about four and a half feet apart, depending on your height. Start to the right of the first Frisbee and do a continuous series of figure eights in between the Frisbees. When you reach the last, turn around and go back. Take short steps on your toes as you weave in and out. Go as quickly and for as long as you can until you're exhausted.

The Bare Minimum Not everyone has the time or the equipment for the extensive program I've just outlined so I'm suggesting a miniprogram that should take only twenty minutes a day. But even with this shortened routine you should swim or relax one day a week to let your body rest.

Push-ups—Start at three-quarters capacity and increase by one a week. Your goal should be three sets of one hundred push-ups.

Sit-ups—Start at three-quarters capacity and increase by one a week with your goal three sets of one hundred sit-ups.

Pull-ups—Start at three-quarters capacity and increase by one every three weeks with three sets of fifteen your goal.

Parallel bar dips—Start at three-quarters capacity and increase by one every two weeks with your goal three sets of twenty-five dips.

Keep at it. It's one thing to talk about the benefits of conditioning and it's quite another to put the theories into practice. No conditioning program is going to get you in shape until you are willing to put enough time and effort into it.

One way to stop yourself from getting discouraged is to use the baby ox theory. If you can't lift a full-grown ox, you should still be able to lift a baby ox. Lift it every day, and by the time the baby ox is fully grown you will be able to lift it. In other words, start with a goal that you know you can achieve and work toward that goal until you are in better shape than you ever thought possible. Believe me, it works.

12

All About
Your Gear

Racquetball is still a relatively inexpensive sport, particularly in terms of the equipment you'll need. It's perfectly possible to equip yourself for less than a hundred dollars for social play; even the competitive player, who needs to equip himself with the best in racquetball gear, can do so for less than two hundred. Be warned, though, that getting the best equipment for your game is not just a matter of laying out the loot. We're all different when it comes to playing this game and that applies to your gear, too. It's worth spending some time selecting the right racquets and shoes—and also for the accessories, which can make playing life much easier for you.

Your Racquet

With the exploding growth of the game, racquet makers have produced a bewildering array of weapons for everyone from the greenest of novices up to the toughest of pros. It's tough to know where to look for good advice when you go to buy a new racquet. I will give you some of my ideas on the subject, but the final decision is yours; I can't stress too strongly the idea of playtesting a racquet before you plunk down the green.

When you are considering buying a new racquet, go to the pro shop or sporting goods store that will loan you a demonstrator model or two so you can get the feel of the racquet. Work your way through several demo models to narrow down the choice of both material and style before you make your final selection. Some stores may charge you a couple of dollars rental for the demo, but that's a good investment, particularly if you can get the rental deducted when you make your purchase.

Incidentally, I think it's best to buy your equipment from your club's pro shop or a high-quality sporting goods store. You may be paying top dollar in such places, but you'll also be getting service if you ever have to take the item back or are unhappy with it in any way. And of course, the advice of a competent teaching pro or club manager can save you from making some costly mistakes.

Types of Racquets Where do you start in your choice of a racquet? The first step is to decide on the frame material. You can choose graphite, fiberglass, metal, or wood. This may be your most difficult decision. Much depends on your style of play and perhaps the type of racquet you've been using.

Graphite's a relative newcomer to the racquetball field, although it's long been used in golf and tennis.

A Graphite Racquet

Graphite fibers are very light in weight but extremely strong along their length. When braided together and molded with an epoxy resin, graphite fibers make a very strong but light racquet. For the power game this combination of light weight and great strength is unbeatable. Graphite is very expensive, however, and so are the racquets. Unless you are a regular tournament player with a power game, I doubt that you'd want to lay out the $150 or so that a decent graphite racquet would cost.

The two most popular materials for racquetball racquets are fiberglass and aluminum alloys. Fiberglass racquets are made from fibers molded with a resin, as are graphite racquets, but the playing results are quite different. Fiberglass racquets are much more flexible than either graphite or aluminum racquets. However, fiberglass racquets are relatively fragile and often shatter when they come into violent contact with an immovable object—such as a court wall.

An Aluminum Racquet

Many top pros favor fiberglass racquets because they are light—for that fast swing—and because the flex of the racquet lets the ball stay on the strings for a longer time and so gives more control. The latter point is somewhat arguable and probably depends on how hard you hit the ball. If you are not a hard-hitter, I doubt that a fiberglass racquet will give you more control than a good metal one.

Aluminum racquets tend to be stiffer than fiberglass racquets, although this quality is dependent on the type of extrusion used. Some extrusions are very stiff; others have a flexibility comparable to fiberglass. Metal racquets are durable, however, and will put up with a lot of punishment. That's important for the beginner and the improving player. I recommend that you start with a metal racquet and then investigate fiberglass as your game improves. You may well decide to stay with metal.

Fiberglass and aluminum racquets are comparable

in cost. Around fifty dollars should buy you an excellent racquet in either material. You'll probably pay more for a model with a famous name—like mine—on the frame but don't be fooled by appearances. Check how the racquet plays in your hands. A top-name racquet does not come with a guarantee for a top-name power backhand.

The other alternative frame material is wood. In the early days of the sport, most racquets were made of wood, but these were heavy clunkers that often fell apart under heavy use. Those models have rightfully been dumped in the nearest wood stove. However, wood racquets have recently been making a bit of a comeback, although I doubt that they will challenge the dominance of aluminum and fiberglass.

The newer wood models are made with laminations, often with fiberglass or graphite reinforcements; consequently, they are stronger and lighter than the historic models. They are also more durable and relatively inexpensive. You may want to consider a wood model if you do not have a particularly powerful game.

Grip Size, Weight, and Balance

In addition to the frame material, there are three factors to consider—grip size, weight, and balance. It's like buying a suit—there are certain measurements that have to be made to get a good fit.

Grip size is not as critical in racquetball as in tennis, because the shorter-handled racquet is less likely to twist in your hand on off-center hits. So I suggest that you choose a racquet with a grip that your fingers can comfortably encircle. This will probably be about two sizes smaller than the grip of your tennis racquet.

There are no standard ways of describing a racquetball grip. Some makers offer small, medium, and large grips, others small and standard sizes, while others use the inch-sizing method common to tennis racquets. The standard or medium size is usually about 4⅜ inches, and this is the grip that most men will prefer to use. The small size is usually 4 inches, and this is the size most women will use.

The grip shape may be octagonal or may be flatter on the sides parallel with the strings. Grip shape is largely a matter of personal preference. Try demos with different handle shapes to see which you like best. Likewise, the selection of a rubber or a leather grip is a personal matter. Leather grips last longer and are more cushioned but have a tendency to get slick with sweat.

Racquets range in weight from 225 to 300 grams, with the majority in the medium weight range of 240 to 280 grams. A light racquet is easier to swing but may be relatively fragile. A heavy racquet is harder to swing but may help you if you put a lot of spin on the ball. I suggest you look for racquets in the range of 240–260 grams and experiment within that range.

Balance is also important in terms of swing speed. A head-heavy racquet will be harder to swing than a head-light racquet, but it will generate more momentum, so you can hit the ball harder. The choice of head-light, even-balance, or head-heavy depends on your game. A power game often calls for a head-light racquet while a control or spin game might benefit from a head-heavy racquet.

Incidentally, you can fool around with the balance of a racquet by cutting an inch or two off the plastic bumper that protects the head of your racquet. You can also add weight to the head with the kind of lead tape used by golfers (and available in many golf pro shops). I urge you to experiment here, too, since altering the balance can change a racquet's playability quite dramatically.

Virtually all racquetball racquets are factory-strung with nylon string at between 28 and 32 pounds of tension. While this tension is fine for most players, I think you ought to experiment with different tensions. You may find that looser strings (below 28 pounds) give more control while tensions above 32 pounds make the racquet feel stiffer and often give more power if you hit the ball hard.

Stringing Your Racquet

You may even want to have two or three racquets and have each one strung at a different tension so you can change racquets if you have to alter your playing style in a match. Just the operation of changing your racquet ostentatiously in a time-out may psychologically demoralize your opponent.

Eventually, your strings will either wear out and break or they will lose tension to the point where you have to get a new string job. If only one string breaks, resist the temptation to get that one string repaired. Get the entire racquet restrung. Choose your stringer with care. It may seem a simple matter to string a racquet—it is not. Experience and care are required. If you are not happy with your new string job, don't hesitate to take it back and ask for the job to be redone to your satisfaction.

Racquetball Balls

Racquetballs It's not too long ago that there was only one racquet-ball manufactured—and often not too well at that. Now there are several racquetball makers, and both the quality and selection are much improved. Now you can actually buy a ball that is made for your game rather than having to adapt your game to the ball.

The two major categories are pressurized and nonpressurized. The pressurized ball is bouncier and suits the faster power game, while the nonpressurized ball is slower with less bounce and is more suited to the novice game. Nonpressurized balls last longer than pressurized.

Balls tend to fracture around the seams. A pressurized ball with a small leak is immediately useless, and I would recommend throwing away nonpressurized balls with even a slight crack, since that can affect the bounce characteristics quite significantly. In fact, you should use new balls as often as your pocketbook will allow. Once balls are removed from their pressurized cans, they start to deteriorate. If you can afford the expense, use new balls every time you play.

Any old sneaker will not do for racquetball. Get yourself either a heavy-duty pair of tennis shoes or a pair of racquetball shoes. A couple of shoe makers have models designed for the tough usage of a racquetball court. Not only will these shoes stand up to the wear and tear of play, but they will also support your feet properly in the fast starts and stops. **Racquetball Shoes**

Leather shoes will support your feet better than the canvas variety, but canvas lets your feet breathe easier. Leather uppers are, of course, more expensive but will last longer. Whichever type you prefer, make sure that the inside of the shoe, especially around the heel, is well padded and that the shoe has a good, firm arch support.

Soles of tennis and racquetball shoes are made from either rubber or polyurethane. Rubber gives good traction but tends to wear out relatively quickly. Polyurethane wears better but may give you less traction on a polished wood court floor. Polyurethane is quite hard, so make sure that your soles are double-density—that is, with a softer layer on the inside to cushion your foot.

Fit is the key to most foot problems. Take your time in buying a pair of shoes. Remember that your racquetball shoes will get a harder workout than a pair of casual sneakers. If you are prone to blisters, wear two pairs of socks when you play—and when you buy your shoes. Run up and down in the store in the shoes and

Men's Racquetball Clothing

Women's Racquetball Clothing

make a few sudden starts and stops to test the fit before settling on a pair of shoes. A few moments in the store can spare you much agony out on the court.

Clothing and Accessories

Racquetball clothing used to be the grungiest T-shirt you could find plus a pair of worn-out basketball shorts. Now we have color-coordinated threads that look just as snappy at a resort as on the court. Having the proper clothes can make a difference. If you feel good out there, chances are you'll play that little bit better. So I recommend you get some proper racquetball clothing if you are serious about the sport.

Your clothes should fit properly but be loose enough for plenty of movement. Skintight shirts and shorts may look good, but they are useless on the court. In addition to your basic shirt and shorts, you

Eyeguard (with lens)

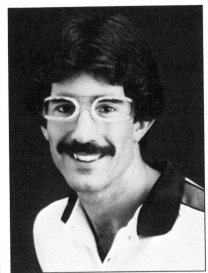
Eyeguard (without lens)

ought to have a warm-up suit, especially if you play in the colder climes where the courts may not be heated to a toasty room temperature. A warm-up suit is useful, too, for cooling off or if you have to make a quick exit without getting a shower.

Your two most important racquetball accessories are eyeguards and a glove. An eyeguard is a must—no ifs, ands, or buts about it. Whether you are a beginner or a pro, and whether you wear eyeglasses (or contacts) or not, you need an eyeguard every time you play. Eye injuries from either the ball or a racquet are a real problem in racquetball. In fact almost 25 percent of all pros have had an eye injury at one time or another. Virtually all those injuries could have been prevented with eyeguards.

If you wear glasses to play, make sure that the lenses are shatterproof and the frame is plastic. You might consider the use of an eyeguard that covers the glasses completely as a further safety move.

Full Glove for Racquet Hand

Eyeguards are mandatory at some clubs—a trend that may be on the increase. Anyone who has suffered even temporary loss of vision knows how serious the consequences of an eye injury can be. Get yourself an eyeguard.

On the other hand, so to speak, gloves are an option but one that I feel is absolutely necessary. Not only does a glove prevent the racquet from slipping in your hand, but it also improves the feel of the racquet and consequently your feel for the ball. There are two types of glove—the full glove and the half-fingered. The choice is a matter of personal preference; I prefer a half glove because it lets my hand breathe more easily.

Buy two or three gloves and wash them often to stop them from becoming slick and cruddy. Gloves will wear out, of course, with frequent play and washing, but they are a relatively inexpensive accessory.

Finally, you will probably need some wristbands and headbands to absorb sweat. Get several of each and change them often during a match, as they become saturated with sweat. You might also get a small towel that you can tuck into your shorts. Use the towel to wipe off your racquet and yourself from time to time. Of course, you'll probably need a bag to put all this gear in. That's up to you, but a bag beats wrapping it all up in a damp towel.

When you play in a tournament, check out your gear well before your match. Make sure the extra gloves and wristbands are in the bag. I also carry a spare pair of shoelaces and a first-aid kit. Having the right gear can add to your confidence before you go out on court.

Index

Ceiling balls, 31–32, 51–52ff., 56 (*See also* Doubles;
    Styles of play); the rabbit and, 82–83
Center-court theory, 6, 7, 61, 62, 68; and doubles, 102–6,
    122; and the shootist, 83–84
Clothing, 156–59
Coil-and-recoil theory, 35–36, 37
Conditioning, 9, 137–45; minimum, 144–45; strength,
    141–44; stretching, 139–40
Crack serves, 28–29
Crosscourt, gambling on, 68–69
Crowder, the, 86–87
Crowding, 72

Deep angle-crack serve, 28–29
Deep spin serve, 27
Deep zone, 62–63
Deep Z serve, 18
Defensive ceiling shot. *See* Ceiling balls
Delaney, Ann, 124
Dell, Fleming, 52
Diagonal defense, 101, 103, 119
Dinker, the, 89–91
Doubles, 7–8, 97–113; advanced play, 112–13; center-
    court theory, 102–6; combinations, 106–11; mixed,
    115–24; formations, 100; and morale, 98–99
Down-the-line shots, 64. *See also* Drive down the line
Drive-and-fly serve, 24–25
Drive down the line, 18–19

Eastern grip, 45, 46
Evert, Chris, 31–32